Whispers of the
DOLPHIN HEART

AN ORACLE OF DIVINE CONNECTION

ANGELA HARTFIELD

ILLUSTRATED BY
EKATERINA GOLOVANOVA

WHISPERS OF THE DOLPHIN HEART
AN ORACLE OF DIVINE CONNECTION

Copyright © 2024 Angela Hartfield
Artwork Copyright © 2024 Ekaterina Golovanova

All rights reserved. Other than for personal use, no part of these cards or this book may be reproduced in any way, in whole or part, without the written consent of the copyright holder or publisher. These cards are intended for spiritual and emotional guidance only. They are not intended to replace medical assistance or treatment. The views and opinions expressed by the author, both within and outside of this publication, do not necessarily reflect the views of the publisher.

Published by Blue Angel Publishing®
10 Trafford Court, Wheelers Hill,
Victoria, Australia 3150
E-mail: info@blueangelonline.com
Website: www.blueangelonline.com

Editors: Peter Loupelis and Cherise Asmah

Blue Angel Publishing would like to thank Angela Hartfield's daughter, Ally Thompson, for her invaluable assitance in finalising this manuscript for publication.

Blue Angel is a registered trademark of Blue Angel Gallery Pty Ltd.

ISBN: 978-1-922574-19-0

Table of Contents

THE HEART OF THE DOLPHIN CONNECTION 7

Tides of Insight: Using This Guidebook 13
Whispers Unveiled: How to Use the Deck 14
Sounding the Depths: Using Your Oracle Cards 15
Charting Your Course: Dive into Divination 18

CARD MEANINGS

1. Celestial Awakening 24
2. Ambient Rays 27
3. Authentic Spirit 30
4. Entering New Dimensions 33
5. Outside Interference 36
6. Retreat 39
7. Abundance 42
8. Wish Fulfillment 44
9. Entrainment 47
10. Open Channel 50
11. Migration 52
12. Sentient Intelligence 55
13. Expansion 58
14. Distant Shores 61
15. Come Up for Air 64
16. Harmonic Vibration 67
17. Anchoring Light 70
18. Low Tide 73

19. High Surf 75
20. Uniting with Your Origin: Dolphin Matrix Chakra 78
21. Connecting to Earth 81
22. Assurance 84
23. Flexibility 87
24. Spirited 90
25. Giving Absolute Love 93
26. Loving Acceptance of All People 96
27. Self-Expression 99
28. Cultivation of Wisdom 102
29. Acknowledging the Divine 105
30. Access Your Enlightenment 108
31. Surprise Encounter 111
32. Taking It All In 114
33. Deep Plunge 117
34. Bubbles of Protection 120
35. Unforeseen Storms 123
36. Light Body 126
37. Auric Energy 129
38. Play 132
39. Dream Time Visitor 135
40. Sacred Water 138
41. Joyous Vortex 141
42. Ride the Wave 144
43. Timing 147
44. Trust 150

AFTERWORD 155

ABOUT THE AUTHOR 158
ABOUT THE ARTIST 160

THE HEART OF THE DOLPHIN CONNECTION

During times of uncertainty,

connecting with dolphins is vital. Everyone experiences fear and anxiety. Fear is a form of stress and happens when you feel like you are in survival mode. It can become harmful when it becomes an automatic response to the environment or people around you. Clearing away fear allows you to receive your blessings and gifts from the Divine.

Dolphins have captivated people's hearts for thousands of years, not only for their intelligence but also for their connection to humanity and our shared history in the astral realms. They are intelligent, sentient beings here on the planet to assist us in shifting into higher frequencies and experiencing true joy and profound love.

Stories relate how the ancestors of the African tribe, the Dogon, came from Mande, an area in southwest Mali and northeast Guinea that was home to the thirteenth-century Mali Empire. After the empire's downfall, the Dogon journeyed to the bluffs of the Bandiagara highlands.

Here, the tribe conveyed the legend of the Nummo twins — unpleasant-looking creatures who arrived in a craft along with fire and rumbling thunder. The Nummo were described as reptilian or fish-like and could live on land but dwelled mostly in the sea. It was from the Nummo that the Dogon claimed their knowledge of the heavens.

The Nummo were said to have come to Earth to provide humans with knowledge. They allegedly gave the Dogon information about their solar system that would eventually be proven centuries later. Hundreds of years before Galileo's discoveries, the Dogon identified Jupiter's moons and the rings of Saturn. They understood that the center of the solar system was the Sun. They have stories about the Big Bang and other astronomical events.

The Dogon asserted a third star, Ęmmę Ya, resided in the Sirius system. Greater and brighter than Sirius B, this star also orbited around Sirius. Around Ęmmę Ya orbited a planet from which the Nummo came. This invisible companion star orbiting Sirius was not identified until the late twentieth century. To this day, it mystifies some that a primordial race allegedly knew of solar systems that cannot be perceived without the aid of high-powered telescopes.

The Nummo's home planet is mainly warm, turquoise-blue water. As such, this race of astral beings takes the physical forms of cetaceans — air-breathing mammals of the sea such as dolphins, whales, mermaids, and mermen. It is said that many of them walk upright and are acknowledged for their innovative use of sound. Dolphins are thus extremely advanced intellectual beings from the Sirius system and are on Earth to support humanity in ways that are well beyond our present understanding and imagination. These beings perform numerous roles, the most important of which is securing the light of the ocean waters. It is thought they hold the keys to ancient wisdom as they were present during the time Lemuria sank into the ocean.

Water that dolphins have swum in is considered to be very healing. When dolphins swim, the healing energy in their aura fills the water they pass through with extra ions, aiding in clearing and healing the mind and body. They demonstrate their dominance of breath and how it stimulates deep emotional stability and alignment of our natural rhythms and harmonies. Dolphin energy encourages us to exhale suppressed emotions and inhale balance, peace, and calm. Water signifies emotions, and plunging deep into the water represents the complexity of those feelings.

Dolphins network straightforwardly with the living core of the earth and the light of humanity's collective consciousness. The mindfulness of this sacred cetacean has an ageless and eternal descent. They are here to emerge a crystalline frequency explicitly intended to shift energies and convert the harmonics of the planet.

Dolphins are distinct souls showing up in the physical realm. Individually they radiate positive energy. They are also naturally adept at synergistically combining their energies. An enormous assembly network within the pods throughout the world's oceans emanates waves of pure golden light. The range of this energetic vibration is limitless. When the dolphin pod moves as one, they produce valuable energies for Mother Earth and humankind. Additionally, when dolphins leap, jump, and spin, they create joyous energy vortexes with the combined unity of the entire pod. This brings balance and continued shifts within the earth.

This deck has been conceived to embody the heart of the dolphins. The intention held during the creation of this oracle is to share with you the profusion of joy, love, healing, and caring given freely by dolphins.

Allow a moment to immerse yourself in our oceans' sacred waters where the dolphins play, sleep, and eat. Imagine being surrounded by their pure love, knowledge, and healing. Feel this exquisite energy permeate your soul, heart, and entire being and radiate from your heart to everyone around you. Trust that the dolphins are here to bring you a higher understanding and alter your vibration to align with the Divine.

Tides of Insight: Using This Guidebook

This guidebook provides interpretations of each card in the deck. Check the table of contents at the beginning of this guidebook to find the page that contains the meaning of the card you have picked, as they are listed numerically.

As you read the dolphins' message on each card, consider it in the context of your reading. Pay attention to any gut feelings or additional thoughts you might have, as these are clues to what the card means for you. Be sure to also look at the dolphins featured on each card and imagine yourself connecting to them energetically. Use your intuition to discover the message that being has for you.

This deck is here to help you connect with the beauty, knowledge, and presence dolphins have to share. Reflect on how the messages and descriptions relate to your questions and situations as you use the cards.

Whispers Unveiled: How to Use the Deck

Oracle cards are an ancient tool for connecting with the Universe's messages. These cards are safe and created with the highest of intentions. Always know that these are your cards. They are not meant for anyone else to handle other than you. The messages you will attract will be for you and are based on the Law of Attraction.

The cards you draw match your energetic vibration at that moment. You may find that you will get the exact same card several times. This lets you know that the message is consistent with what you need to know at this point.

Oracle cards are helpful because they directly link you with what you would benefit from knowing. When you find yourself in a stressful time, these magical dolphin cards will help you see your situation from a higher perspective and gain a greater understanding by revealing pathways to help you navigate this moment.

Sounding the Depths: Using Your Oracle Cards

CLEAR YOUR CARDS

Your cards are sensitive to vibrations and may have taken in unwanted energy during manufacturing. You may want to clear your cards before receiving the information you seek.

Hold the cards in your non-dominant hand—the hand you don't write with—over your heart. You may close your eyes and consider your intention while working with this deck. Take a deep breath and feel your energy imbuing your deck. Feel gratitude, knowing it will help to give you insight into and clarity on your questions. Once you have done this, turn the deck over and look at the cards. Begin to familiarize yourself with the images on your oracle cards. Look at each card individually, then give the deck a good shuffle. This process is part of the personal initialization to instill your energy into the cards. You are getting to know your cards and feeling comfortable with them.

Use and interpret the cards in a way that feels right for you. Read the guidebook to see if the message answers what you need to know. Don't feel like you must be dependent on the guidebook. Trust what you are feeling. Each card will represent something specific to you, which could have an entirely different meaning if you read the card for someone else. You will soon start integrating your intuitive mind with the knowledge of the cards and messages of wisdom for your interpretation. Keep a journal of notes to help you gain deeper insight.

Make your deck sacred to you. Some people wrap their cards in silk or store them in a special box. Treat your cards with respect and love.

PREPARING YOURSELF

When you are ready, take out the cards. Hold them in your hands, close your eyes, and center yourself by taking a few deep breaths as you clear your mind. Shuffle the cards to impart your energy to them.

ASK A QUESTION

After you have shuffled your deck several times, think of a question you are willing to hear the truth about. If you are reading the cards for someone else, have them ask out loud or silently a question to which they would like the answer. Trust that you do not need to hear their question to draw a card and give them an answer.

SHUFFLE THE CARDS

Once you have asked a question, reshuffle the cards and pay attention to what feelings you begin to receive. You may notice thoughts, sounds, or visions concerning the question you are asking. Stop shuffling when you feel the time is right. It may be that the cards feel different or that you are compelled to stop. There is no right or wrong. You will stop shuffling at the perfect time for you.

CHOOSE A CARD

You may either choose a card from the top of the deck, or you may decide to cut the deck and look at the card in the middle.

Once you have selected a card, take some time to look at the picture. Notice any thoughts or impressions that you have regarding the card. Then look up the card meaning in this guidebook. Allow yourself to receive the card's love and guidance.

Charting Your Course: Dive into Divination

THE THREE-CARD SPREAD

This is a standard card spread. Its purpose is to clarify what is going on in your present, its roots in the past, and a possible consequence that lies in the future.

Shuffle the cards and place the cards face down, left to right (see diagram below). As you turn each card over, ask for the information coinciding with the aspect the card represents. Sometimes it is a good idea to start with the second card (the present) to orient the context of your reading.

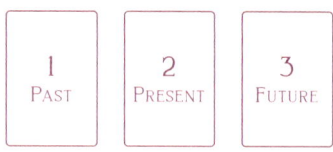

Card One: Past — The roots of your current situation.
Card Two: Present — The current factors and suggested steps to take.
Card Three: Future — Possible consequences should nothing change in the present.

THE WHIRLPOOL SPREAD: FINDING YOUR INNATE GIFTS

The purpose of this spread is to assist you with discovering your soul's true nature. The different positions of the spread show the areas of your life that you may choose to foster or explore further.

Shuffle your cards and lay them out face down in an outward-turning spiral, as shown in the diagram below. As you turn the cards over one at a time, ask the question that correlates with the card placement.

Card One: What builds my confidence?
Card Two: What helps me to stay healthy?
Card Three: What gives me a sense of fulfillment?
Card Four: What gives me pride about who I am?
Card Five: What makes me laugh or brings me joy?
Card Six: How can I be kind to others?
Card Seven: How can I support the beauty of others? Also, can be the 'outcome'.

CHAKRA READING SPREAD

The purpose of this reading is to assist you with finding your chakra's message. The spread shows the chakra that needs extra care. There are eleven chakra cards in this deck. They are cards numbered 21 through 31.

1. Separate the eleven chakra cards from the rest of the deck. Shuffle these eleven cards.
2. Once you have shuffled the eleven chakra cards, choose one card and lay it face down according to the card layout format. Set the remaining ten cards aside. You will not use any of the remaining ten chakra cards in this reading.
3. Shuffle your larger pile of cards, draw them, and lay them out face down according to the diagram.
4. As you turn the cards over one at a time, ask the question that correlates with the card placement.

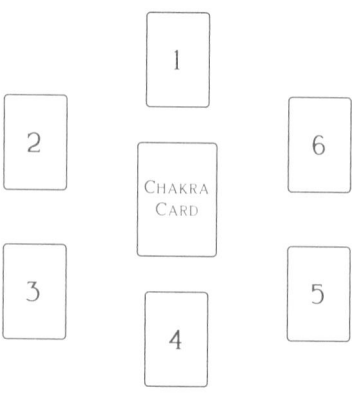

Chakra Card: This is the chakra that currently needs your attention.

Card One: What is this chakra desiring you to do at this time?

Card Two: What communication does this chakra want me to know right now?

Card Three: What is the challenge that needs balancing regarding this chakra?

Card Four: How will I know when this chakra needs extra care in the future?

Card Five: How do I strengthen my relationship with this chakra?

Card Six: Is there anything else I need to know?

CARD MEANINGS

1. Celestial Awakening

Awaken to your spirituality and the life lessons you are destined to learn.

ONLY YOU CAN DECIDE when you are ready to have an impactful spiritual encounter. It is thought that awakenings sometimes happen to help us reconnect to our true celestial nature. This card is telling you that it's happening now. These steps help bring that on and prepare you for a journey of learning, change, and self-discovery.

One of the most straight-forward steps is to start by creating space. Everything holds energy. Rid your environment of unnecessary things that fill your space, collect dust, and distract you from creativity. Eliminating the excess from your life is not limited to your physical surroundings — clear your thoughts and mind.

Commit to spending time each day in seclusion and stillness to sort through the stories running through your mind. Forgive yourself for any past mistakes and allow your thoughts to leave you. Release judgments you may be holding on to, observing how your mind unwinds and clears. When you meditate, allow yourself the opportunity to relax into the truth of a situation. As you calm your mind, fear and pettiness will subside, replaced with love and a stronger connection to your inner guidance.

Now is the time to evaluate your beliefs. Be deliberate and conscious about what it is that you accept as truth. What areas of your life are you expending your energy on? Consider how your beliefs affect your immediate circle and the whole world. Do your current views support your spiritual growth? Letting go of limiting beliefs clears the way for spiritual awakening. To grow your spirituality, clarify what you want to shift and awaken.

Seek ways to expand your mind, such as exploring different philosophies and new ideas. Have conversations with individuals who have lived differently from you, read books or listen to podcasts. Spiritual awakening occurs when you rouse your spirit and mind by learning something new. Expanding your consciousness will allow new ideas and opportunities to take hold. As you grow, you raise the possibility of waking up to life experiences you did not realize existed.

Turn off your devices and find gardens, trees, or parks with fresh air. Imagine a beautiful oceanscape beckoning to you. Allow yourself the quiet, solitude, and presence of nature and the outdoors. As you engage with your inner peace, the space you have created within may surprise you as it emerges into your conscious mind and outer world.

Taking better care of yourself keeps you linked to your Source — God, Spirit, or however you identify it. Prioritize your self-care, eat smart, and make an effort to stay active. You block your spiritual growth and awakening when inappropriate habits slow your well-being. Keep yourself healthy and clean. Eat well, move well, and be open to the answers you pursue.

Dolphins are keepers of ancient energy, otherworldly magic, and the spirit of joy. Connect to the beauty of dolphins and the ocean. Take some time to reconnect with nature. You may be in a city, but there are ways to connect with nature, the sea, and dolphins.

As with most things in life, you can't force your spiritual awakening. There are no exact or guaranteed steps that lead to your enlightenment. Be mindful and release the need to know when. You will impede your progress if you become attached to your spiritual awakening. Trust that the path you are on is the perfect path for you.

You are not limited to a one-time spiritual awakening. Your spiritual path is continuous. Staying on track will lend the opportunities to awaken to deeper consciousness and new awareness throughout your life's journey.

2. Ambient Rays

CONTINUOUS SPIRITUAL light rays descend on you from the heavenly realms of the stars, the planets, the Universe, and the Creator — even if you are unaware of them. These rays are the essence of love and peace and exist infinitely in the timeless realms of higher dimensions. These higher dimensions have different modes of environmental laws, rhythms, and patterns associated with them.

In prayer, meditation, and other spiritual practices, you can elevate your frequencies into these higher dimensions of light, bringing peace, comfort, and protection. You may even perceive a golden ray of light shimmering in your inner eye or the room around you. Prayers travel on these light rays creating a telepathic synergy between subject and object. As prayers telepathically move across these light rays, they are received via the upper energy centers (chakras). However, when

Hidden worlds become visible when you connect to the ambient light rays of the ocean. You will experience harmony, unconditional love, and contentment.

your mind is occupied with repetitive and negative thinking and your upper chakras are blocked, your thoughts act like static interference. Any messages intended for you aren't received or are distorted and unclear.

This card tells you to clear your mind of inner noise and become an open channel. Silencing the mind chatter is the key to seeing these light rays. To do this, close your eyes and breathe deep into your abdomen. Slowing your breath helps you breathe deeper. Imagine the breath filling up the area below the belly button, and only let your thoughts focus on this task. Stray thoughts will inevitably arise — acknowledge that they are there, let them go like a feather on the breeze, and return your attention to the slow, deep breathing rhythm. If it helps, call on a dolphin guide to assist you, imagining yourself in the ocean with them.

Having silenced the mind, you will be open to whatever you receive from the ambient rays around you. When you get past the limited thinking and antiquated perceptions that keep you stuck in a three-dimensional experience, you will be able to see the multicolored light rays that fall on and emanate from all living beings. The psychic vibrational love connecting to your higher self will stream down to your three-dimensional self and bless you with resilience, new ideas, and opportunities for growth and healing.

As you modify your vibrational frequency and shift dimensions, your brain waves move into a theta state—the place between conscious and subconscious thought—accessing the ambient rays. At first, you may see a glimmer of an aura or the appearance of a white-light outline around a plant or some other life form. If you have seen dolphins in the water, you may have seen the white trail of light radiating from them while they swim. Ambient light may be visible after deep meditation, sitting quietly in nature, or swimming in the ocean with cetaceans.

Dolphins can see these light rays that swathe every conscious and emotional being in existence. Very young children often see these light rays too. The secret of a child's ability to see imperceivable light rays lies in living without the intrusion of constant chatter. Beyond your thoughts and concepts are the realms of the higher dimensions.

These light rays assist you with feeling the comfort, love, and peace that is always there for you. It takes time to develop your gift to see the light. Allow yourself to unwind and break old thought patterns. Meditative, calming music can help with opening your higher-dimensional sight. Awareness of light rays teaches you a lot about energy dynamics in the environment. With time and practice, you can understand the nature of the patterns around you.

3. Authentic Spirit

Your authentic spirit is your true essence and intrinsic nature. Staying connected to universal and sacred inner knowing is joyful and liberating.

EVERYONE HAS AN authentic spirit that lies in the center of their being and can never be changed or taken away — it can only ever be hidden and covered with remnants of social, familial, and cultural conditioning.

When you encounter the energy and essence of someone new in your life, you can become enamored with them. To you, they appear grounded, self-realized, and possessing traits you admire or desire to develop in yourself. Later you realize they are not who you thought they were, falling from your grace when you discover them engaging in disreputable, thoughtless, or insensitive behavior. What you are finding are the flaws of the conditioned self, not the true nature of that person. You blame yourself for allowing yourself to be tricked. Why did you perceive this person or group in such an unadulterated way? It could be that you are naïve, or it could be that you are learning about the inherent flaws of being a three-dimensional human. What you are discovering is that the possibility of imbalanced growth is inescapable in every individual.

The genuine essence of a person is already perfect and filled with light. The energy can be spacious and gorgeous. Some aspects of our behavior may impair this essential nature due to experiences of painful trauma or less-than-ideal childhood development. This can be confusing because you think someone is a beautiful person, but later they may surprise or offend you with what seems to be an offensive break of personality.

We need to be considerate and sensitive to the authentic spirit of a person when we relate with others. You are encouraged not to be critical of your colleagues, friends, family members, or others, including yourself. This card guides you to gradually develop discernment by looking at things objectively and clearly through experience. This process requires time and effort. A person's true nature is obscured due to masks and learned behavior patterns. Discernment comes from listening to your intuition and acknowledging your authentic spirit.

Stand back and gain perspective — you can see that these hurtful actions are unintegrated and unrefined aspects of personality and patterns covering the authentic spirit, like surface debris over amazing, brilliant light. The soul is still untainted. Eventually, the truth of the genuine essence will burn away the debris of a lifetime of conditioning. Each being is set with its divine timing and blooming. You cannot rush, push, or alter someone else's development. Learn to compassionately accept the immature aspects of behavior in your friends, family, and even yourself. See, feel, and love their true spirit and energy as well as yours. Stand in the light of your spirit and intensify your luminosity.

Dolphins don't have preconceived notions concerning who they are. They are not preoccupied with self-image — they are already authentic, unpretentious, and spontaneous. Dolphins are not concerned with skin color, height, appearance, and weight. They are natural and manifest their fundamental nature at all times. These sacred creatures show you how to stay connected to your true spirit and let go of all the judgments or disillusionments you may have. Follow the example of the dolphins, express your authentic nature, and recognize that same spirit within those you encounter daily.

4. Entering New Dimensions

THE DYNAMICS OF EARTH are constantly changing. As the planet accelerates in frequency and the intensity of life is sensed more deeply, this card is a clear message to pursue new ways to cope with higher stress levels. You must learn to match the higher vibrational frequencies and prepare yourself for the new dimension of existence.

There seems to be amplified drama, crisis, and extreme emotions in people and circumstances around you. You feel like you're losing control and have little or no space to recapture your energy between intense situations, challenges, or emotional upheavals. Your sensitivity is increasing rapidly, and managing your vulnerable feelings is now overwhelming.

As the planet alters its frequency toward a new wave of awareness, the people, animals, and plants become a microcosmic replication of the earth. They

Move into a place of greater clarity, multidimensional understanding, and amplified sensitivity, and receive the higher levels of consciousness that are now becoming accessible.

are also growing in frequency and power. The ever-changing energy will present a challenging time for those who resist the upward spiral of life and energy. Things will become more uncomfortable physically, emotionally, and spiritually. Anger, anxiety, and depression may become more apparent.

When you are ready to enter new dimensions, open your mind by releasing old fears. Allow yourself to dwell quietly in the crystal-clear understanding of your physical mind, which interrupts your notions concerning everything. You will then see things around you from a new perspective. Learn to regulate your physical body through breathwork, movement, and any embodiment practice appropriate for you. Utilize mindfulness techniques that help you mentally cope with the potentially overwhelming influx of energy and information. Above all, trust that if you are hearing this call to a higher level of consciousness, it is because you are ready and able to achieve it.

Dolphins are ultra-sensitive beings and often become ill in confined and unnatural environments. They need to dive deeply, spin, jump, play, and have the open sea to swim in. These activities are how the dolphins sustain clear energy channels, eliminate stress, and stay happy and healthy. Look to them as an example of how to cope with the changes that are currently underway. They want to share their coping mechanisms to assist you with the ascent into the higher dimensions.

With this energy, your dolphin guides show you how you are moving quickly through cycles of expansion and contraction. Where there is calamity or chaos, you contract with pain and stress. As the crisis is solved or released, there is an expansion and self-liberation of your entire being. This flux is swift and continual. Learning to adapt to it and match the vibration leads you to gain numerous attributes such as mindfulness, added clearness, insight, finer tuning of judgment, greater intuition and clairvoyance, and growing compassion.

5. Outside Interference

Disruptions do the most significant damage— or interfere with you —when you permit their presence to affect you long after you have returned to your original project or task.

EVERYBODY EXPERIENCES outside interference — you are not different from anyone else. We can become irritated when our creative flow is interrupted and frustrated when structured measures don't go as scheduled. Interruptions to your flow can feel jarring, making you resent yourself for your inability to avoid distractions and feel like interference is a sign of personal weakness. You may also view distractions as a change in your journey instead of a shift beyond your control. This card is a reminder that disruption is part of life, but how you deal with it is the measure of success.

This is a time for you to pay attention. You are often warned ahead of time by your inner guidance whenever problems lurk ahead. Sometimes advice is very subtle. Disruptions or issues may lie in your path, but for your best outcome, listen quietly for guidance as to what you should do. When you are energetically aligned, you enable your intuition to reach out and find the best advice. You often receive very subtle callings. These more minor signs are usually right in front of you. A straightforward manner to receive communication from the Divine is through your dreams. Pay attention to these — many religions consider them one of the principal means to relay information to you from the Divine.

Sitting in stillness can also assist you with divine guidance. Perhaps you're hoping to hear advice, but you are afraid you will get it wrong. Become clear about what you are seeking direction for. For example, is it your well-being, finances, love, or work situation? Song lyrics that you hear repeatedly may have a message for you. A conversation you overhear could be a message meant for you. Magazine covers with topics about something you are interested in or announcements on billboards are also ways that messages show up for you.

When you listen with your heart, you will continuously be guided in a way that assists you in navigating any external blocks on your path. Who you are now is shaped by following those persistent whispers and how you adapt to disruptions out of your control. In the realm of signs and symbols, guidance opens to show you messages through synchronicity and nature. Attentiveness, relaxation, and becoming still when in the outdoors will open your mind and heart to your inner guidance. Symbols and signs will show up repeatedly until you recognize what they signify for you.

Sometimes disruption is so significant that the only way forward is to leave this path altogether. You may have been on a road you believed was your purpose — don't despair, however. Each person has hundreds of callings in their life. Some callings are significant, while others are small. Rather than one life purpose or mission, you have many prospects to practice qualities of whatever makes you feel alive.

Dolphins will form alliances with other pods in harmony to avoid conflicts. The message here is to be aware of any subtle guidance surrounding you, and ask for help from guides like dolphins do with other pods.

See the presence of outside interference as a blessing in disguise. Use your values as a guide. These are the virtues that make you who you are. Create a record, or journal your primary beliefs. How are you respecting those beliefs in your life? What evidence do your principles give you about your calling? How do you deal with the presence of blocks and interference on your journey? Living your life by revering your callings creates profound serenity and a more energetic world for you to experience. Pay attention to your guidance and see where your callings take you.

6. Retreat

THERE ARE TIMES WHEN a retreat is necessary. Maybe you feel like a fighter who has been beaten. Soldiers retreat from the frontline to mend their injuries, recover lost energy, and evaluate what transpired. Spend time with yourself without fear of whatever may come up in your thoughts or emotions. Whether you stay at home or travel far away, taking this time for yourself allows you time for a valuable assessment of your deeper self.

Over-commitment and a packed schedule disconnect you from your inner knowing and guidance. There are times when you become drained from excessive stress. You can get out of alignment with your fundamental well-being when you push too hard in your daily life without taking a break. Sometimes you are forced to pause because of burnout or illness. This can often turn out to be a blessing in

It is time to move away from your daily routine to take a short respite.

disguise. This is particularly true if you utilize your downtime as a retreat. Meditation and self-reflection help you reestablish a life of stability.

Your self-perception is formed by your past experiences, position in life, work responsibility, gender, and how your family and friends see you. When you retreat, your self-image begins to dissolve. You are stripped of your self-image by removing yourself from your reactionary behaviors and coping mechanisms. When you do this, you open to depths within yourself that you may not have realized are there.

The prosperity of your consciousness and the spacious quality of your mind has an opportunity to soar uninhibited to explore possibilities for your life. Joy and laughter appear like a spring of sparkling, vibrant water uncontaminated by social conditions. If you are connecting with nature on your retreat, you may feel so merged with it that you feel the life force tingling in each cell of your body. When you are cleared, your life force can flow freely and enliven you. By giving yourself the opportunity, you become aware of the things that ordinarily rob you of your life force.

There are times when dolphins may retreat from their pod. Dolphins are considered adept energy managers and clearers. Just as you may experience times where you feel overloaded, a dolphin will also withdraw from its routine to clear its energy and recenter. To do this, dolphins suddenly burst across the ocean in a power swim, repeatedly jump for joy, or race aimlessly amongst other pod members. Often, you may notice a dolphin swimming slowly by itself as if it has entered a meditative state. Once they have cleared any stagnant energy, they rejoin the pod refreshed, harmonized, and ready to hunt or play.

Each of us has a unique formula for keeping the life force flowing through our lives. Specific relationships sometimes take too much out of you and drain your energy, so give yourself sufficient seclusion for inner reflection to recharge your batteries. Maybe you need to change your profession to the one you enjoy. Sometimes, it is a simple matter of reordering or reprioritizing how you relate with others. It may also be how you manage the mundane details of your life. Consider keeping a journal. Write down all your dreams and make lists of your goals and affirmations. Whatever the situation is for you, dolphins have swum into your cards to remind you to have some form of retreat to reset your nervous system and get your life force flowing freely once again.

7. Abundance

Abundance begins with developing a way to exist in your everyday life by utilizing the gifts you already have and accomplishing the objectives and goals you love.

THIS CARD DEMONSTRATES that you have taken steps toward evolving to a place of generosity. Bigheartedness in all of its forms comes back to you tenfold. Whatever energy you put out in the world will come back in a variety of manners. It isn't that being generous creates abundance. It is when you become open-hearted and giving that it becomes part of your nature. This shift opens nature's flow of abundant energy to surround you.

In addition to money, abundance comes in a multitude of forms. Humans and animals have lived abundantly on the earth for millions of years. They gave to the planet and took from it only what was needed. There was a balance to the equilibrium of giving and taking that allowed abundance to flow freely.

Abundance does not flow from a feeling of lack but out of energy that circulates love and the spirit of giving and receiving. Energy in motion sustains abundance and healthy well-being, but stagnant energy leads to feelings of fear, worry, illness, and lack. Grasping tenaciously to what you have, or fearing its loss, tends to slow down the abundant flow of energy. Feelings of resentment, feeling forgotten, or as if your life does not matter cause energy flow to stagnate. This stagnation begins to affect your capacity to attract, and you may find that you vacillate between a sense of fear/lack and the belief in your ability to receive.

On the other hand, feeling connected to the world around you and everything in it changes how you attract abundance. When your energy is flowing, doors open for you and provide direction, means, and answers to how to create the life you desire. Once you realize your worthiness to receive and focus on your positive intentions, abundance begins to flow naturally. Relax and believe in your worth and your beautiful light. The Universe gifts abundance to every single living creature. When you truly give from a place of love and open your heart to receive what you need and desire, the Universe will send blessings of abundance to you.

Dolphins show you the ease of the flow of abundance. Nature provides dolphins with all their necessities. They live in freedom; they know they are worthy of eating every day and enjoying swimming and playing. They exude the quintessence of happiness, joy, and abundance. Watching or imagining them helps you to remember that the Creator made you worthy of abundance and love. Your only job is to open your heart and receive. You are enough.

8. Wish Fulfillment

When you extend a silent prayer from an open heart and unlimited mind with total faith and confidence, the opportunity for wishes to be fulfilled is at hand.

WISHING FOR SOMETHING is one thing; fulfilling that wish is another. It's not unusual to have dreams and goals and feel disheartened when we can't see those outcomes fulfilled. We can become despondent when we feel like we can never win. There is an art to fulfilling your wishes, and this card's lesson is how to make them come true.

Find inspiration through your dreams, ideas, and goals — what is it about what you want that is so important to you? Ask yourself, "What do I want this for?" Be proficient at honestly evaluating yourself. How aware are you of your strengths and weaknesses? Are you good at keeping deadlines or with follow-through? Answering these questions benefits you so you can assess whether or not you are progressing toward your goal. Sometimes you can get off track. You may not even be aware that you aren't progressing, and it takes someone else to redirect you back on course. Conversely, if you can honestly assess how you are tracking and accept what caused you to become distracted, you can give yourself the scope you need to change your target and wish.

Maybe you need to reorganize your objective. This doesn't mean you are facing a setback or failing. Revisions to your desires, adjustments, and shifts along the way enable you to grow and eventually reach your goals. Changing your wish means understanding your aspirations and integrating new knowledge for a superior outcome. Dare to refresh your dream if needed.

Additionally, you might have to forgo something to reach your dreams. For example, if you want to exercise more often, you must make time somewhere throughout your day. Or, if you would like to add a wholesome breakfast to your dietary routine, you may need to rearrange your morning to create the time to eat properly.

Release your attention from your wish and focus your attention elsewhere. Bringing light and joy into someone else's life can bring light into your own life. Remember the adage that when you give to others, you also receive. When you lose yourself in being of service to others, you shift your fortune. This allows the Universe to conspire on your behalf and bring your wishes to fruition.

Dolphins live their lives with joy. Despite obstacles, they live trusting that whatever they need will be provided. They fulfill whatever they desire without the preoccupation of trying to achieve anything because they have faith and open hearts.

When we follow their example, we set our desires, get on with life, and adapt to whatever comes our way. When this card appears in your readings, it is a reminder that setting a goal also requires checking in from time to time on whether that goal is relevant and having faith that we will receive whatever we need to. The more you see your blessings surrounding you, the more blessings are bestowed upon you.

9. Entrainment

ENTRAINMENT IS THE activity by which two diverse techniques come into harmonization. For example, it occurs when two similar structures come together, such as when you place two grandfather clocks in the same room — initially, the pendulums will swing autonomously. Over time, the plumbs come to waver in synch. This organization materializes through pulsations in the atmosphere and the flooring.

This synchronization (entrainment) in connecting with dolphins will enrich your life. When you allow your energy to shift to the same frequency as dolphins, you may experience a feeling of increased clarity, vitality, and energy.

Dolphins innately live in a status of hemispheric brain management — they have to since they are sentient creatures. They breathe with breaks, meaning they

Dolphins utilize their frequency to entrain you by linking you to their energy.

swim under the water for approximately four minutes and then break the surface for breath. On the other hand, humans live in an atmosphere of air. We can breathe deliberately or focus our attention elsewhere and breathe unconsciously. But dolphins can't operate this way and do not rest as we do. They have to stay conscious enough to ensure they stay awake to breathe. They do this by shutting down one brain hemisphere and using the other in a method comparable to how we use one hemisphere or the other for our waking activities.

But when dolphins are conscious, they instinctively use both sides of their brains simultaneously. A dolphin's natural brain state is comparable to our optimum state. Because dolphin brainwaves are far more intelligible than ours, we naturally entrain to their frequencies when exposed to their sonar pulses. Dolphins use these sonar pulsations to interact with and investigate their environment. When in the presence of dolphins, their vibrations pass through our body like a medical ultrasound, permeating every cell in our being and synchronizing us to their more comprehensible frequencies.

When this card appears in your reading, it asks you to become swept into the dolphins' energetic flow and feel heavenly and peaceful as they surround you. Go swimming with dolphins and become more entrained in their state of consciousness the more time you spend in their company. And that exposure is cumulative, making it increasingly easy to enter into and sustain similar states of consciousness, even when you are not in the water.

If you cannot physically swim amongst them, find yourself recordings of dolphin sounds. Listen to these while meditating, and allow the sonar pulses to harmonize your consciousness to theirs. You could also practice breathing through alternate nostrils while you meditate, a yogic practice called *nadi shodana*. Similarly, do activities that activate both hemispheres of your brain and get them to work simultaneously, such as cross-lateral movements (like crawling), mismatched movements (rub tummy and pat head), or juggling.

Attune to the frequency of dolphins, and you will shift to their elevated realization of playfulness and joy. By activating both hemispheres and operating at an optimum level, we are more equipped to move through our world with effortlessness and grace.

18. Open Channel

Allow yourself to open your heart, mind, and body as a conduit to divine love, healing, protection, and guidance.

YOUR GUIDES ARE sending you messages. To effectively receive this guidance, it's essential to practice becoming an open spiritual channel. This involves embracing the clarity, wisdom, and skillfulness necessary to be a divine conduit. Proficiency, understanding, and lucidity naturally flow when you embody this role.

When seeking guidance, the best way to be an open channel is to be grounded. Grounding helps you focus, grasp sustained energy, and connect to your authentic self. It also supports energy stabilizing more quickly once you have completed your channeling and connecting.

After grounding, imagine your heart filling with the light of the Universe and visualize it mixing with the energy of your authentic self. It is easier to be an open channel once your energy has expanded, so allow your heart to remain in this dynamic. Anchor your energy while envisioning where you want to connect with your guidance. This can be anywhere: a favorite place, feeling, memory, crystal, or color.

You may sense your guides nearby and be aware of sensations in your body. Once the energy has built up sufficiently, you can initiate channeling outwardly by vocalising or writing and bringing through the utmost divine and seamless guidance for yourself or others. These are inspiring moments. The information that comes through during this phase is meant to be used. You are seeking answers, and the Universe is giving you a clear message.

As an open channel, you can sit in meditation and become so deeply relaxed that any tension you may be holding in your body is released. You may feel the awakening or opening to peace flowing throughout your body. It permeates and comforts every cell in your body.

As open channels, dolphins see through that radiant doorway to the Divine as they swim Earth's waterways, spreading their playful joy. Dolphins also need open channels to survive predators and fishing nets. They share that information through clicks and high-frequency communication if there is a clear, safe passageway in the ocean. It is vital for their survival and the survival of their pod that they are clear and open to receiving all information.

By remaining grounded and connected with your authentic self and the Universe, you will be the open channel you and your community need.

11. Migration

Change can show up in several ways. You can move from where you are, alter your current approach, or open your mind to new possibilities.

WHEN WE THINK OF THE word 'migration', we often use it concerning animals or birds. Examples are sea turtles who return to their original nesting grounds each year to lay eggs or geese flying north in the spring and south in the fall. Some species of dolphins are known to migrate seasonally, moving to warmer waters in the cooler months and returning. In the animal kingdom, migrations are a response to a deep, instinctual urge to make changes vital for a community to thrive. When this card appears in your reading, it is time for a shift — and it may not be physical.

Migrating back and forth between two or more homes at different seasons of the year is reminiscent of how our hunting-and-gathering ancestors lived. Our ancestors followed the seasons and the food, migrating to specific locations for the resources they needed to survive. The movement of non-sedentary peoples was their way of ensuring that nature's bounty was not depleted in any one place.

When you feel a compelling, primal movement inside of yourself to change something in your life, your body's wisdom and inner knowing may be uprooting you and guiding you to the next chapter of your destiny. It may involve moving to a different city or country for a new job that will be more fulfilling for you. Or it may simply be changing schools to one that offers something more aligned with your goals. It may even be moving to warmer climates during the winter for health reasons. Whatever the case, you are being called to make a migration that will benefit you right now.

Of course, there are logistics to take care of. How will this affect your everyday routine? How will it affect those closest to you? Are you leaving behind your roots and networks of support, and will you be able to re-establish those elsewhere? Nowadays, businesses and the military create migrations for people transferring away from their initial homes. This transfer disrupts established networks of support. In the past, the extended family would typically migrate together to enable them to eat and survive with other family members. If you are going to make such a significant change, you will need to attend to these details that will impact your well-being and that of others.

Another form of migration is the ability to shift your mind from a long outdated viewpoint. Just like when our ancestors stayed in one place, an opinion or a belief may have used up all the resources you need to grow and thrive. It's okay to change your ideas about how the world works when the ideas you have held onto no longer work for you. You can remove from your mind all you have learned before and migrate to a fresh, clear view.

     Migrating can change your perceptions of the reality you live in. Rearranging your routines will shift your habits. Changing your surroundings can alter your energy and open up your mind. When you alter your old, long-held thoughts, you open yourself to a new way of thinking. Migration to a new awareness illuminates your life with light. This awareness is the initial step to enlightenment.

12. Sentient Intelligence

WHEN YOU FUNCTION AT minor or lower stages of your consciousness, you feel disengaged, bored, preoccupied, unfocused, unimaginative, or unmotivated. This mind frame can benefit certain circumstances, such as controlling tedious undertakings. Yet even in those instances, optimum levels of awareness—or mindfulness—could improve your understanding, so you are more expressive. When this card shows up for you, it tells you to develop 'sentient intelligence' — the higher level of awareness that comes from the linked conscious and unconscious minds.

Individuals often inaccurately confuse mindfulness for egocentrism and directing attention to oneself. Your rational mind is continually seeking inner chatter and replay of conversations. You may look for things to watch, become part of, or use distractions to entertain yourself and preoccupy

Sentient intelligence is mindfulness in a continuum that streams from an unconscious mode to total awareness.

your conscious mind. In truth, sentient intelligence means carefully considering those around you and your environment. It means concentrating on what's occurring in the present moment.

Scientists examining dolphin demeanor have proposed that these sea mammals could be the most intelligent creatures on the earth behind humanity. Dolphin behavior suggests complex higher-order intelligence. It is currently thought that even as non-humans, dolphins may deserve to be given the rights of individuals.

Developmental studies indicate that dolphins, especially bottlenose dolphins, have distinctive personalities and self-awareness. Dolphins can contemplate the impending time ahead. The investigation also established that dolphins have multifaceted community arrangements, with specific dolphins being assigned the role of co-operating to decipher problematic difficulties or to gather up shoals of fish to eat. Moreover, they have the dormant ability to pass on new or learned behavior to other dolphins. The spiritual nature of the dolphin has a deep understanding of something beyond the rational; mindful that there is a higher plan and a consciousness not usually considered.

Two simple factors are involved with entering that state: posture and breath. Changing our posture to maintain a straight spine, open chest, and loose limbs allows for neurological and circulatory free-flow, directed by abdominal breathing (using the diaphragm to open the chest downwards, instead of shallow breathing with shoulders opening the lungs upwards). Generally, this is normal when we feel relaxed and stress-free, rather than anxious and tight.

Another factor is engaging our peripheral vision rather than focal vision. This technique appears to widen our visual field and activates a more acute sense of hearing. Allowing our minds to engage with the world around us and be present eliminates (or at least minimizes) the distractions of inner chatter. Engage with the world around you with curiosity and wonder, rather than boredom, and show an interest in everything—no matter how seemingly mundane—that enters your field. Trust that your unconscious mind will process everything it needs and feed that information back to your conscious mind when necessary. Use your capacity to feel to adopt the nature of the dolphin.

Developing your sentient intelligence means keeping your conscious mind open enough to access information already held in the unconscious mind instantly. Sustaining a higher level of awareness will help you when confronted with a full timetable and avoid sliding into a preoccupied mode, which can be problematic on many levels.

13. Expansion

Embrace new experiences, skills, and an open heart to become a more magnetic and compassionate individual.

YOU EXPAND INTO A well-rounded individual when you discover new things, cultivate new skills, or showcase an undeveloped gift.

Your energy field contracts when you are afraid, worried, or irritated. Conversely, when you feel happy and secure and share wholesome, loving energy with others, your energy expands around yourself. The dolphin of expansion has swum into your reading, telling you to find ways to grow into the magnificent being you indeed are.

You contract when you feel invisible, lost, unattractive, or unimportant, but expanded energy is magnetic and attractive to others. Learn techniques to clear stagnant energy from your field and instead generate a positive, outgoing, friendly vibe. Everyone may not see an expanded aura, but it will be felt. We are usually attracted to open, expansive individuals. These people are often described as charismatic, dynamic, friendly, attractive, or having a magical presence.

You may have realized there is more to your life than how much power or material wealth you can accumulate. These things grow in number, but your soul doesn't expand accordingly. Work on increasing and staying open. This is an opportune time to look around and see if you can better serve others in the world around you. You have an opportunity to give. When you give, do so without the need to be recognized for your deeds. The ego is challenged when doing something for someone else without expecting something in return. Expansion is truly learning to be of service from the heart space without the need for accolades or acknowledgment.

Consider expanding your mind by learning something new. Maybe enroll in a short course in something you're fascinated with, a language or musical instrument. Perhaps you'd like to learn a new skill, like carpentry or painting. Learning is an excellent way for our brains to refresh and keep growing — intellectually or physically. It will help you expand your experience of the world around you. It will also develop your consciousness of different aspects of your being and discover a part of yourself you never knew existed.

Expanding your heart and spirit will help you heal your wounds. When you grow your heart, you have more room for others' love and will undoubtedly have more love to give. You may become so raised that you develop the ability to see auras around people. You often have clear perceptions or clairvoyance when you are highly expanded. These skills are helpful when you turn your wound into the source of your power to aid others similarly affected.

Dolphins are inherently curious and will appropriately approach and explore when something new enters their environment. Emulating this behavior can lead you to discover people and places you would typically never encounter. Work out where you want to expand your life and set out in that direction — you never know what you'll find.

14. Distant Shores

THIS CARD EMERGES FROM the deck when you find yourself feeling like you are stuck in a rut. No matter what you do, nothing seems to shift or change, and your routine is monotonous and feels like there is no progress in your life. Now is the time to disrupt your usual pattern and head for distant shores.

When we find ourselves in these situations, it is usually because we are so set in our ways that we close ourselves off to new information and ideas. Everything you contemplate, say, and accomplish is filtered through your upbringing. Conditioning is learned in the family unit and also from society. We are rarely conscious of how our basic assumptions are pre-formed, so it's easy to shut down our receptivity to different ways of looking at the world. Without this, our creativity is stagnant. The answer is to seek out something different.

There is a thrill in seeing new places and leaving your everyday life behind.

When you seek different experiences, be open to the guidance that allows things to unfold without the need to control every aspect. Think outside of the box, and look beyond your usual culture. You may feel drawn to a culture or tradition you feel connected to. This may involve learning a foreign language, trying a new cuisine, traveling to an exotic place or simply learning all about it. When we immerse ourselves in a culture different from ours, we start to see and think more broadly and examine everyday life through different lenses. Recognize that a part of you is feeling called to connect with this new interest. It's calling you for some reason.

Dolphins are related to one another across the world. They circle the earth's ocean, diffusing messages of unity, peace, and harmony as a community of love. A dolphin may not see all their relatives on the near-distant shores, but they are in communication through their collective consciousness, sonar, and telepathy.

When you allow your world to open up, watch how new opportunities, unique individuals, and auspicious connections flow into your life. Traveling gives you ample opportunities for a change in direction, with many magical meetings along the way. Learning about different cultures, traditions, cuisines, and customs brings diversity and enrichment into your life. Your mundane life and daily routine have been left at home. You have leaped the trajectory into uncharted waters and the free flow of the magical world.

There are many rewards for you when you seek out the unknown. You can form trustworthy relationships with others and build connections between what you already know and what you still need to learn. With more knowledge and more experience, you can select behaviors, materials, and ideas that help you grow and still honor individual cultures and life experiences. These are the skills we all need to develop to succeed in a global society.

15. Come Up for Air

Relaxation is the key to developing intuition and greater awareness.

BREATH IS LIFE; WITHOUT it, mammals would die — including ocean-dwelling cetaceans like dolphins. It also plays a part in regulating our nervous system. When you draw this card in a reading, your dolphin allies are reminding you that a calm nervous system is what you need right now so you can move through life with greater awareness.

Dolphins are constantly aware of the importance of the breath because they are often underwater and need to gauge their time. Similarly, taking deep, abdominal breaths can assist you in relaxing. This card is a gentle reminder that the things you tend to worry about may never come to fruition. By relaxing, you release the energy of a stagnant situation. You see positive and harmonious events flow when you relinquish control of problems and others.

Watching dolphins can bring about relaxation. Dolphins gracefully swim, spin, play, and jump without creating tension or feelings of stress or exhaustion. Sometimes the relaxed state opens you up to meditation, and you can balance your energetic body. When you're calm, your health is enhanced. If you do have a health condition, it has a better opportunity to return to a normal state. Being in a state of chronic tension can lead to health problems. Excessive tension releases chemicals that wear down your body's immune system.

Stress is your body and brain's way of relaying that you must be alert and on the lookout. It is a low-grade, perpetual state of fight-or-flight. To handle your stress more effectively, begin by acknowledging your feelings. It doesn't matter what the feelings are. By bringing your conscious attention to them, you will dissipate them easier. Activities like journaling, exercising, visualization, doodling, or engaging in something you enjoy are positive ways to deal with stress. This allows your brain the opportunity to reset.

Positive thinking can do miraculous good for your mental well-being. Make an effort to alter the manner in which you mentally speak to yourself. Stop minimizing yourself and try to replace your negative thought patterns with positive ones. Positive affirmations are a tool that can assist you in changing your attitude about your life. They are potent declarations intended to expand your convictions and change your mindset to a positive one.

Perceptive influences happen in a mind that is accessible and relaxed. Many individuals get their best insights and perception when doing something mindless. Some of these activities include everyday chores, such as washing dishes, taking a shower, or other activities that you participate in without having to think about them.

It isn't natural for you to be constantly on the go with your body in a perpetually tense state. Block out some time in your busy schedule to come up for air. Give your brain time to reset. Remember to breathe and calm your nervous system so that you can be as stress-free as possible and allow the insights from your intuitive self to shine through.

16. Harmonic Vibration

ANY TIME YOU FEEL 'OFF' and cannot put it down to illness or stress, it is because you are being bombarded by vibrations that are not in harmony with you. This is a common occurrence, and luckily your dolphin allies have appeared before you to show you the way to a harmonic way of life.

Harmonic vibrations relate to the science and art found in the dolphin realm and musical sound. Harmonics can relate to feelings, energy, actions, and ideas in addition to music. Dolphins' sounds, tones, and songs are an example of the harmonics of these marine mammals that have not been completely understood or deciphered by scientists and marine biologists.

Different sounds in nature generate their harmonic vibration. The rhythm of pounding waves, the sound of the wind, the call of birds' songs and the chattering and

Listening and bringing your full attention and presence to the harmonic vibration around you is the key to creating an open flow of understanding.

clicking of dolphins swimming in the open ocean create a unique harmony that soothes your soul. No matter what environment you find yourself in, nature delivers the harmonic soundtrack that elevates you vibrationally.

Harmonics relates to more than music, sounds, or nature. Harmonic vibration is found in shapes, textures, sizes, colors, proportions, words, and art. People have seen geometrical shapes when meditating, relaxing to classical music, or any music with harmonic progression. You may even find ways to move your body that harmonize with your hearing and feeling. Look for harmonies in artworks and design. You will know because you feel at peace in the space.

Harmonic dissonance can cause your system to go into an emotional imbalance or physical abnormality. Imagine the sound made when you strum a guitar whose strings are out of tune. This happens to us when we are out of tune with our surroundings. Often, the city's noise—cars honking horns, loud noises, yelling, or discordant music—creates chaos and is disharmonious to your heartbeat and natural rhythm. It can also be about the people and ideas you are surrounded by — the negativity of the daily news, the dissonant images on your social media feed, or the yelling of your neighbors. These will all contribute to feeling out of sorts.

Just as musical progression is layered with expressions and rhythms, take some time to find the rhythms layered in nature. Listening and bringing your full attention and presence to the harmonic vibration around you is the key to creating an open flow of understanding. Allow your heart to reharmonize with the rhythms and harmonies found in the natural environment.

You can find recordings of nature sounds on an app or elsewhere if the real thing is not readily available.

Make your home harmonious by decorating it to generate vibrations aligned with the body, heart, and soul. Re-arrange the furniture, and utilize colors, artworks, and even sounds to make your home a respite from the outside noise. Pay attention to the media you're exposed to. Read books composed of beautiful words with ideas and stories that raise your vibration. You may even want to learn more about Feng Shui and Building Biology.

Make an effort to reset your energy. Shift your harmonic vibration to help you stay clear, healthy, and balanced, and this will lead to a greater perception of the subtleties of life.

17. Anchoring Light

Anchoring light relates to utilizing your own divine, distinctive light that resides within you.

WHEN YOU DRAW THIS card, it is telling you to bring your light into your everyday reality. Express it mindfully and acknowledge this manifestation of who you are. There is a necessity, particularly during times of amplified challenges or anguish, to have access to a divine resource for connecting to your soul's true identity, so that any difficulties can be resolved from a place of openness found within. This light needs to be anchored into physical reality to serve as a connection point for you in challenging times.

Countless beings have felt an awareness of solitude over lifespans due to the estrangement inherent in physical manifestation. By the configuration of the human brain and nervous system, the embodiment of an eternal soul creates the perception of separation. The inner knowing that all is held in God alters this separation. It allows the outer self to connect with the innermost truth, to individualize and feel that no matter the struggle, one's inner self is protected and secure.

The difficulty in accessing your spiritual anchor lies in the drive to seek out our desires on a superficial level. This is challenging for the authentic self because the body—which contains both cerebral interests and emotions—can feel the intensity of pain. You become convinced that the feeling of pain is the only thing that is real. While on a spiritual level, you are trying to shift to an enlightened belief that Higher Source is your actual reality.

The conversion of consciousness from the exterior perception to innermost experience can dissipate the limiting hold of material reality on one's mindfulness, even when uncomfortable circumstances occur. It can rearrange the focus of awareness to a profound place inside you where optimism, hope, faith, and love reside and where trust in the future lingers.

Thus, the purpose of anchoring your light is to dismiss this mistaken idea that only what exists 'out there' is real and generate the consciousness that God and love are the actual reality. This is even true in times of challenges, doubt, and fear.

Having such an anchored connection is not a skill but a way of communicating an inner knowing that everything is held by a Higher Source (Spirit, God, etc.) — including the events that are testing your will. This acceptance is the difference between progressing through a difficult moment with an awareness of being supported versus moving through the same circumstance with a sense of despair and feeling lost and alone.

Dolphins anchor light to the ocean floor. They do this effortlessly by emanating light from their heart chakra to the bottom of the ocean. Entire light grids have been built and connected by dolphins circling the planet, drawing in and anchoring light energy to the ocean's floor. The actual light work they have done has created the dolphin matrix chakra. This is found approximately seven feet below your feet, beneath the earth's surface. Further beneath the dolphin matrix chakra is the whale matrix chakra. This chakra has also been created from the light and sound work done by the ocean's whales.

The practice of anchoring light can be performed in various ways. You may anchor to your light through mindful breathing, praying, engaging in meditation practice or other healing modalities. However you choose, anchoring light aligns the process of shifting the outer self to the inner, from the pain of the external situation to the peace of the soul. It also allows individual consciousness to separate itself more fully from whatever interpretation that collective opinion places on your situation, allowing one's inner truth to gain ascendance.

18. Low Tide

When the tides are out, or the surf is calm, you can gaze into the tide pools of sea life, typically covered by the ocean during high tide. Tide pools are small ecosystems of life that are unique to themselves. When not much seems to be happening on the exterior of your life, this is a time when you are in low tide.

This may occur when you are between relationships, projects, or jobs. It may mean that you are in a transition period in your life or in a place where your energetic flow has slowed. Your social life may not be a priority. It could be that friends may be out of town or too busy to connect with you. You can be in a phase where your friends move on or no longer seem to harmonize with you. You might be sorting through your friendships to determine which friends resonate with the new you. You may have already decided that self-centered,

Low tide in your life may represent a time when not too much seems to be happening on the external level.

harmful, or draining relationships are no longer something you choose to engage with. You may have to set up new boundaries for old relationships. You might even have to end old associations. The outcome is to honor yourself and keep your energy protected and harmonized.

    The dolphins have waded through the shallows to remind you that this slow period in your life allows you time to pause and regroup. You may need to disconnect from everyone and everything you know to reconnect and discover more about yourself. Taking a break to recalibrate and regroup is necessary to stay on track with your personal growth. When you remain dedicated to routine, there is a good chance you may stagnate. Living up to the expectations of others is based on who you once were. It is challenging to become who you aspire to be when stuck in the expectation of what others think you should do.

    When the ocean is calm, and the tide is low, dolphins find retreat in the bays. This enables them to swim meditatively, using only half of their brain for swimming while they regroup and rest. Slowing down allows time for inner growth. Let this time be for preparation before high tide brings new energy, opportunity, or an exciting phase.

19. High Surf

HIGH SURF IS characterized by sheer power — large waves crashing onto reefs and shores and the ocean bristling with unbridled energy. There is no mistaking the might of the seas when they are in this phase. Pulling this card in a reading signifies that high surf is surging, and it's time for you to harness that energy for your creative purposes.

Dolphins recognize the period of high surf as a time of high energy and opportunity. During a high surf phase, others may also be trying to help boost your energy. Respect this time as you may not be fully adept at handling it. Even the dolphins know to rely on their strength and power while respecting the energy of the high surf.

When you are in a time of creativity, knowing your most important goals helps you ride the waves easier because you are aware of your direction. Knowing what

High surf can point to a period of great excitement, unlimited happiness, or passions teeming with the energy of new love or creative expression.

you want and what you want it for will undoubtedly lead to success on your part. Please take advantage of the energy swirling around you in these phases and harness them to accomplish your dreams.

Taking care of others is a basic necessity for your happiness. When you help other people feel better or cared for, it is not only for their benefit, but it will help you to feel happier and healthier. In moments of high surf, there is plenty of energy to give you what you need and share with those needing your assistance. When you give, it creates a stronger relationship between people and helps to build a happier association for everyone. It is not always about financial gain; you can give your ideas, energy, and time. Positive relationships are the most important overall contributor to happiness. People with strong and broad social relationships are happier, healthier, and live longer. Close familial relationships and strong friendships offer love, meaning, and support and increase your feelings of self-worth. Larger groups and associations can convey a sense of belonging and being part of something. Taking action to improve relationships and produce new influences is vital for bliss. This is something we can learn from dolphins and their social structures of cooperative pods.

How often do you stop and reflect on the world around you? If you have thought that there has to be more to your life, you can discover it by taking a moment to be more aware and mindful. Being more attentive is marvelous for your well-being in all aspects of your life. Take a walk at lunchtime, or spend some time with someone you care about. Get more in tune with your emotions and decide to finally stop obsessing about the past or planning for the future. The high surf phase means you have excess energy to perform this simple act, which will help you get more out of your everyday living.

Have you tried anything new or unusual to keep things fresh in your life? In moments of high surf, you can be supported to take opportunities you wouldn't usually be able to. For example, learning something new affects your well-being in various and positive manners. It exposes you to new ideas and lets you stay engaged with the world and curious about what is happening around you. It may give you a sense of satisfaction, resilience, or completion and can boost your self-confidence. There are numerous ways to perpetuate your learning. Simply taking the time to venture out and engage in something different can lead to a world of discovery waiting for you to find it.

The surf is up, and now is your time to take advantage of it and find how you can ride the waves to what you most need in your life right now.

20. Uniting with Your Origin: Dolphin Matrix Chakra

Each person has a dolphin matrix chakra located a short distance from your physical body beneath your feet, below the earth star chakra.

THE DOLPHIN MATRIX chakra is approximately six feet under the earth star chakra. It familiarizes you with the central star and connects you to the energy of the dolphins, assisting you to feel more grounded and connected to Mother Earth. Dolphins have much wisdom stored in their pineal glands. They wish to assist and guide individuals ready to remove and release the blockages accumulated in this part of the brain. The dolphin matrix chakra specifically supports and activates any new changes in your light-body field and your DNA.

If negative energies and influences are left to accrue, you might feel blocked from your telepathic dreams, visions, and the growth of your auric energy. Dolphins want to acclimate you to the predominant star matrix, which is kept within the genetic makeup of their brains. They ultimately aspire to reconnect you to your higher self while connecting to your pineal gland. This will enable you to recollect the purified ancient wisdom of previous civilizations.

The star beings—including whales and dolphins—are giving you the opportunity to work with them to receive information downloads. It is one of the most harmonized systems, allowing you to benefit and gain information about memories and intelligence you may have forgotten. When the dolphin matrix chakra is cleared and balanced, it generates the inner knowing that you have been in a slumber and are beginning to awaken. This chakra can assist with recalling the perception and certainty that you hold within your being. After developing a connection with the dolphin matrix chakra, it becomes easier to determine when the seven main chakras in your physical body are out of alignment and need balancing and harmonizing.

Working with the dolphin matrix chakra will prepare you to transition into a more meaningful existence. Dolphins are the only beings on earth with three frontal lobes, while humans have two. This third frontal section is believed to be the area of the brain that helps dolphins have a resilient relationship with each other, functioning in harmony and insight.

Dolphins also have a highly established intuition. The stimulus that causes an attraction to the dolphins is that your body is over 70 percent water. The dolphins are now calling you back to your origins, your authentic nature. They want to escort you tenderly and lovingly on your journey of cleaning, corresponding, harmonizing, and realigning your chakras to assist you in understanding your complete reality.

A straightforward way to connect with the dolphin matrix chakra is to stand barefoot, close your eyes, and breathe deeply from your abdomen. Once you feel centered and grounded, imagine a connection from your body to the area roughly six feet below the earth's surface. Once you feel connected, imagine the light grid this chakra connects you to, and see or feel how it spans across the entire planet, maintained as it is by the dolphins. This is your connection to Mother Earth. Notice what you see, feel, hear, and experience. Use this knowledge to live in harmony with the natural environment.

Connect with the dolphin matrix chakra and reunite your soul with your dolphin allies, helping each other to maintain the light grid around the globe. By doing so, you aid all beings on the planet and yourself.

21. Connecting to Earth

It's essential to be aware of the importance of the earth's energy, especially when connected to how countless people live on the planet. Various individuals have disregarded the earth star chakra for a long time. These days, people rarely take the opportunity to walk barefoot and consciously connect to the earth. This contrasts with our ancestors, who were often barefoot, taking the time to honor the world and its abundance of blessings.

The earth star chakra is situated approximately 12–18 inches underneath the soles of your feet. The purpose of this chakra is to support celestial energy to be correctly substantiated and anchored into the terrestrial sphere. Unlike other chakras, it is not located within the physical body but is part of the auric association. By consistently discharging surplus energy down through

The earth star chakra is principally correlated with creating a relationship with the earth. It is intended to help ground your energy into the earth's core.

your root chakra into the earth, you avoid numerous health concerns produced by being ungrounded. If you seldom create a connection and instead devote time to using mechanisms that bring abnormal energy into your existence, you may quickly develop discord in your life. This chakra establishes an alignment between you and the earth's magnetic core and unites you with Mother Gaia. When cherished, it is believed to safeguard the continuation of pristine well-being.

This chakra's significance is how it spiritually roots your bodily chakra system to the earth through your foundation (the root or base chakra). It helps regulate the energy concentrations in your body and enables you to remain present in daily existence. It is particularly essential for everyone that this chakra is positive and harmonized, and spiritual people need to utilize it to help them remain grounded.

The earth star chakra represents the relationship between your physical body and the earth. Feeling love and appreciation for Mother Earth and for everything she provides is the way we maintain the health and integrity of the planet. If we and all other species of life are to remain living on Earth sustainably, then being grateful for our planetary home is a critical step in preventing her from becoming unlivable.

This chakra is where you anchor your physical being and vitality to the earth. As you respond to the earth's dynamism, you achieve objectives. The earth provides a nurturing environment for you to 'plant seeds' that enable the growth of your creativity while feeling connected to life around you.

Dolphins are very present beings. Their connection to the earth is vital to the communities they live in. Dolphins must use their instincts and connections to nature in order to survive. They must be present and aware.

The earth star chakra reminds you to ground and find your connections to your body, to your circle, and to the collective. Stand or walk on the earth barefoot. Go for a walk or a hike through nature, go camping and spend overnight sleeping on the ground. If that is not pragmatically possible, stand or sit in meditation, breathe deeply into the abdomen, and sense your entire chakra system connecting to the area of the earth star chakra, releasing any negative energy into it and receiving the nurturing pulsations from the earth mother.

Feel yourself become more present and resilient to whatever you need to achieve in your activities today, and use your power to help maintain the integrity of Mother Earth. Be there for her, as she is for you.

22.
Assurance

Looking to others for assurance is helpful, but developing your own support and validation system will bring harmony and balance into your life.

IF YOU FACE A PERSONAL or mental challenge, this card reminds you are not isolated. There is support and love around you. There are resources available to you. This may help you feel less upset, doubtful, afraid, or alone.

Many choices you make intentionally and intuitively touch your consciousness of well-being. For some individuals, feeling secure means having a stable, pleasant job with a respectable salary. For others, reassurance might include emotional well-being, like developing trust in a relationship, or it might signify feeling confident in one's body. Making conscious choices can help generate a more joyous and self-assured life.

While getting assurance from the people around us is good, we also need to develop our unique systems of support and validation. This increases your ability to soothe yourself as you gain inner strength and confidence. One way is to set aside time each day to give yourself some acknowledgment. Recognize the things you've accomplished, steps you've made, the growth you have had, or the time you have taken for yourself. When you habitually commend and encourage yourself, self-support becomes a routine you can rely on when you need it the most.

Expressing your emotions appropriately is a healthy practice. It removes the charge from your feelings and allows you to see the underlying root of your experience. Acknowledging this, you are free to pursue help for genuine difficulties, not your self-judgment over dealing with your emotions' ups and downs.

The card image's dolphin represents the first chakra, located in the pelvic region in the perineum. It is called the root/base chakra, and *muladhara* in Sanskrit. This is the energy center of stability, assurance, safety, and an individual's basic needs. The energies of the root chakra assist you to feel supported, grounded, and connected to Earth, giving you a place for your life to take root and for the flow of energies to propel you forward on your life journey. It is said to resonate with the color red.

When the root chakra is open and balanced, you feel confident in your ability to withstand challenges and stand on your own two feet. When it's blocked, you feel exposed, as if you're standing tenuously on an unstable or crumbling foundation.

When working toward establishing confidence for your root chakra, the first step is in moments where you could use some reassurance. You may need reassurance when choosing, encountering a new task, facing an emotional issue, or dealing with depression or other mental concerns. When you find yourself in this situation, heal your root chakra by making choices for yourself based on growth, maturity, and spiritual development.

When we think of the dolphin, we think of joyous animals rooted in ancient wisdom and custom. Dolphins share their social behaviors passed down from mother to calf to create their culture. Thus, the dolphin reminds us to balance the root chakra through connecting to what makes us feel at home.

You have a right to happiness, health, joy, and creative existence. Your root chakra will become defined by how you live, love, communicate, and the other choices you make in your life.

23. Flexibility

IN LIFE, TRIALS, challenges, and circumstances will push you to your limits. When you fail to adjust to meet the challenges that show up, you may find you are motivated by an attachment to how you thought events would transpire. Opening your sacral chakra enables you to sense the world everywhere and throughout your being, making it easier to adapt to the moment's needs. This makes the sacral chakra vital for the groundwork of your relationships with the world around you.

The sacral chakra, known in Sanskrit as *svadhisthana*, is instrumental in developing flexibility in your life. Connected with the water element, it is characterized by movement and flow in your emotions and thoughts. It supports your expansion, growth, and the development of uniqueness through relating to others and the world.

Modify your present attitude toward your situation to enable you to adapt.

Becoming flexible doesn't happen overnight. Pushing yourself to achieve this too quickly could set you back. As with physical exercise, you can hurt yourself when you overdo it. Instead of doing things in a hurry, start by trying something new gradually. Adjust your current mindset and decide to do things differently, such as choosing a new or unusual place for lunch. Remember the sensation of opening up to something new and different. Keep this feeling in mind; it can get you through any unforeseen change of events or an unexpected invitation.

The sacral chakra oversees the sacrum region, the large pelvis bone between the hip bones. It is associated with emotions, sensuality, intimacy, sexuality, and creativity. When this chakra runs well, your physical body and your emotional life function healthily. The sacral chakra pulsates to the color orange. When the energy moves up from the root chakra into this one, the vitality received motivates your capacity to co-exist happily and contentedly in the world.

This chakra is thought to be more aligned with femininity and the moon. Similar to how the moon instigates the ebb and flow of the ocean's tides, the sacral chakra symbolizes your ability to allow and helps you recognize when you have enough, knowing that you deserve the life you want. Remaining flexible while learning to be grateful for what you have will maintain the ebb and flow of the sacral chakra. By cultivating flexibility, you can channel your energy towards achieving a balanced lifestyle that emphasizes positive emotional expression in your actions and possessions.

Dolphins swim with agility and flexibility in the oceans. They move with ease and grace. This card reminds you to connect to your sacral chakra through movement. You can activate this chakra by bringing your attention to your sacrum while breathing into this area. Imagine an orange glow that spins like a vortex. Sensual dancing and moving hips in slow undulations can help release and move the energy of this chakra. Because of its association with water, spending time in a bath, pool, or the sea also benefits. A balanced sacral chakra will make you feel creative, optimistic, and cheerful.

Follow the flow that emerges from this chakra, and you will notice how easily you can adapt to any situation you find yourself in. Like water, you will be able to find your way past any obstacle and wear away slowly at those you can't.

24. Spirited

Energy, drive, and motivation are fundamental to feeling alive and experiencing happiness.

THE SOLAR PLEXUS chakra, known in Sanskrit as *manipura*, is the warrior's fire that motivates us to achieve. Residing in the upper abdomen near the diaphragm, this region of personal power oversees your ego, personality, individual freedom, choice, and dependability. The solar plexus glows with a brilliant yellow shade. When you draw this card, you must bring attention to this energy center.

When the solar plexus chakra is lacking in fire, you will feel depleted. You will lack the willpower to undertake ordinarily uplifting activities. There is a fear or inability to make decisions, and you don't have any energy to manifest goals. These are all clear signs that this chakra needs to be balanced.

A stable solar plexus chakra constructs the steadiness between your power and congruent connections with others and is integral in maintaining your motivation. Keep your spirits high and understand yourself well and what keeps you motivated. A straightforward technique is to set simple goals and achieve them. Determine what the aim or purpose of your goals are. Establishing clear and concrete intentions concerning what you are working toward can keep you engaged, on track, and in alignment with your solar plexus. As you complete these goals, set newer ones that are slightly more challenging. This way, you increase your resilience bit by bit.

If you feel yourself start to drop again, consider reestablishing what it is you are seeking to gain. When the task of staying motivated feels overwhelming, create a vision that resonates with you clearly and compellingly. Think of the bigger picture but break it into manageable chunks. Harness the power of the solar plexus to emphasize your resolve and accomplish any goal you set out to achieve.

Gut feelings assist you when you are at a crossroads and baffled by choice. If it doesn't align with your true nature, it won't influence you to stay on track. Generate the best visualization possible since you can manifest what you perceive. Take a different approach to the task at hand. Sometimes just getting started might be the problem. A new approach gives you a new perspective and more energy.

Dolphins maintain a balanced solar plexus through their lives' constant movement and steady focus. This is similar for us in that when this chakra is healthy, we have the power to keep on going.

Stay spirited by keeping it optimistic and upbeat. Encouraging thoughts lead to positive actions, and self-affirming assertions will aid you in succeeding at your finest. Take control of how you feel, behave, and think. Positivity will help you make the decisions that will bring you success.

25. Giving Absolute Love

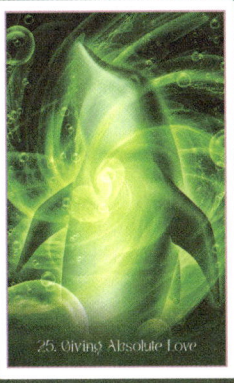

25. Giving Absolute Love

The heart chakra transports love through your life outward to others.

THE HEART CHAKRA, called *anahata* in Sanskrit, is the fountainhead of love, kind-heartedness, consideration, and joy. It is positioned in the center of the torso at the heart level. It is the center of your unfathomable connections with other beings, your consciousness of consideration and compassion, and your feelings of self-love, selflessness, bigheartedness, benevolence, and deference. The heart chakra assimilates and unites, drawing in energy from above and below and transmuting it. Because of the healing aspect of love, this chakra—and the region it inhabits—is seen as a potent healing instrument.

The energy of the heart chakra enables you to realize that you are an integral part of something bigger than you. Along with the sentient beings of the sea—dolphins and whales—you begin to understand that all relationships are held within an intricate network of connections encompassing all life and the Universe. *Anahata* permits you to individualize and be present with this fundamental truth. A meaningful existence comes from a heart focused on love and inter-relatedness.

You channel love, kind-heartedness, friendship, and compassion into your life to benefit others. When your heart is open, it inspires kindness and compassion in others. They can feel your love, warmth, and unconditional acceptance. People sense your integrity — there is no critical opinion or judging. This creates a safe and supportive environment to open one's heart and permits you to appreciate all of the splendor and love around you, creating inter-connectedness between yourself, your loved ones, and the earth. This chakra also supports receiving love, allowing you to love and appreciate who you are genuinely and the physical body that represents you.

A healthy and well-adjusted heart chakra is crucial for your whole well-being. Your heart needs to be uncluttered for free-flowing love, consideration, and understanding. When you feel jammed up or shut down in your heart, you can stabilize this vitality center with uncomplicated approaches such as chanting, meditations or yoga postures that work on the heart chakra. Any stretches that open the chest laterally, combined with breathwork (open chest, breathe in; close chest, breathe out), are also helpful. Even something like singing or dancing to your favorite song will clear your heart and open you to the affection and magnificence encompassing you. Essentially any activity that fills you with joy helps maintain the health of *anahata*.

Dolphins maintain clear and open-hearted chakras by living in an environment that assimilates joy and love. They prioritize the importance of their family and community by keeping play and rest as a part of their daily activities. When this chakra is in harmony, you will connect to all around you and feel like trials and difficulties with social interactions stream over you with simplicity and grace.

26. Loving Acceptance of All People

Acceptance of others is meaningful to achieve a positive existence.

MOST INDIVIDUALS TEND to struggle when it comes to acceptance of others. Human nature often leads us to assume that the speaker knows best, and we can be prone to judgment or criticism. Everyone has moments when they struggle to accept another. This card reminds you to take steps to help you become more tolerant and positive in your relationships.

Monitor your thoughts and recognize what you are dwelling on — are you quietly judging other people? We tend to fall into this type of behavior unconsciously frequently. Shift your thoughts toward being less judgmental and work on being open-minded. Make a deliberate effort to see the good in others. Become conscious of your thoughts as a daily practice.

Staying away from comparisons and seeing things as black/white or right/wrong will also help foster better relationships.

Differences can exist without one having to be noted as wrong. Avoid labeling things and the need for your view to be the only one that is acceptable. Realize differences can coexist, and there is no one way to accomplish something.

Your reproaches of others are an outcome of your perceptions. Stop belittling yourself or re-analyzing your actions and reactions throughout the day. Self-criticism leads to criticism of others. When you stop being critical of others and yourself, you will become more accepting of others. Live in the present moment and look at things from another's point of view. Imagine if someone else was critical of you. How would that feel? Once you change your perspective, you can lovingly accept others.

The thymus chakra—also known as the higher or unified heart or the soul seat—is significant in aiding the concept of self-love, joy, and unconditional love for all humanity. It is the epicenter of loving acceptance of all people, religions, and philosophies, connecting you to the earth and the heavens. It is the bridge between your soul and the world. This is the chakra of connection, peace, attunement, and alignment with everything spiritual.

When the thymus chakra is open, you can accept love and offer it joyfully to everyone. It inspires you to care about and unite with other individuals, generating a grid of relationships that was not imaginable beforehand.

This energy center is positioned above the physical thymus gland, between the heart and throat chakras. It creates a pull of both energies and blending them assists in loving communication between the individual and the soul. This makes it possible for proper guidance to flow through the heart. It also enables caring interaction to move out to the many people experiencing fear, threat, and denial of the changes coming to the earth and the physical body. Only through kind and caring communication can this be done efficiently and inoffensively.

The thymus chakra deals entirely with the connection to angels, ascended masters, spirit guides, your higher self, and higher powers from the dominions of light and love. It permits you to enter your sacred records and activates higher perception, allowing your higher mind to meet your inner child. It can bring belief and spiritual wisdom down from the heavens while keeping you connected to the earth plane.

Dolphins have harmonious societies due to their excellent relationships. One of the lessons they are here to teach humanity is to open our thymus chakra to generate self-love that reciprocates amongst each other. Then we can accept each other for who we are and get on with the more important task of building loving and sharing communities. Following their example, when you accept yourself—flaws and all—you can accept those around you. You will find it uses less energy, making it easier to co-exist with your neighbors.

27. Self-Expression

Sometimes you're uncertain how to retrieve your creativity or know what you want to say but don't know how to. Not speaking your truth can have damaging effects on your self-esteem. Self-expression is the realization of your true spirit and genuine personality, witnessed by others when they see the entirety of who you are. When you clearly express yourself, it is the crucial step in acts of kindness and fundamental for goodwill, contentment, and self-actualization.

Complete self-expression involves taking a leap of faith when needed, living fully, creating options that exalt your wishes and aspirations, and not settling for something less than what you want. You have a divine privilege to be joyful and satisfied, and if you are not, then you have the opportunity to transform.

Self-expression demonstrates your uniqueness, whether utilizing words, your fashion sense, a distinctive hairstyle, or expressing yourself through writing and illustration.

The throat chakra, or *vishuddah* in Sanskrit, is located at the midpoint of the neckline. It is the center of one's self-expression and distinctness. It is responsible for communication, accepting the possibility of different thoughts and concepts, wholesome inner dialogue, and the dynamic between listening and talking. It expresses authenticity and individual honesty. Functioning in unison with your sacral chakra, the throat chakra enables you to direct original thoughts in creative expression instead of repressing them for fear of others' judgments.

A balanced throat chakra assists in giving you unrestricted ability to communicate free from the worry of unwanted opinions or admiration from others. It helps to embrace your uniqueness and distinctive proficiencies in the world. It is also associated with transparency, hence uniting it with the idea of truthfulness.

To become proficient at using your voice and maintain the throat chakra's flow of energy, practice speaking your mind with a trusted person who will listen objectively. If you aren't comfortable sharing your thoughts and opinions, consider journaling your feelings. Any regular self-expression will help care for the throat chakra and enable you to advocate for yourself as you strengthen and balance it continually.

To live authentically, embrace your unique encounters and experiences in the world and appropriately share them with others. Each person has a unique story, and a well-adjusted throat chakra empowers and inspires that contribution. There is not one thing more compelling than communicating your reality.

Living your truth starts with quietening the mind. Mindful breathing is one way to quiet thoughts by concentrating on your breath. As you breathe, focus on the action while only thinking, "Breathe in … breathe out." When other thoughts arise, notice them and allow them to pass peacefully. This exercise is more challenging than it appears but becomes effortless with continued practice. It produces tranquility in your mind, and you begin to relate closely with your authentic self and unlock your throat chakra.

Dolphins have open throat chakras because they swim in pristine turquoise waters. Additionally, they can communicate with each other without the messiness of the ego. Listening to dolphins clicking and chattering with each other can assist you with the opening of your chakra. Imagine how freeing it would be to say whatever you need without worrying about the limitations you have in place. These limitations include how it will be received, the fear of hurting or being abandoned for feeling the way you do, and other concerns that come from a place of fear.

This card's lesson is to speak your truth from a place of love. As you work toward releasing old, antiquated beliefs regarding expressing yourself, the more balanced and open your throat chakra will be.

28. Cultivation of Wisdom

Cultivation of wisdom is acquiring the ability to do the right thing at the right time for the proper purpose.

THE THIRD EYE CHAKRA, or *ajna* in Sanskrit, is located in the center of your brow. It can see both your outer and inner world while recording what transpires. The third eye is responsible for clear thinking, self-reflection, wisdom, and contemplation. In spiritually 'seeing', you may filter the external world and give voice to your inner world with a symbolic language. The message of this card is to begin cultivating your wisdom by balancing this chakra.

Wisdom does not imply you are brighter than others. No one wanders into knowledge — it takes intent, determination, and effort. You will not acquire it instantaneously. It develops gradually throughout everyday life. When cultivating your insight, avoid using it with an inflexible agenda.

The vitality of *ajna* permits you to access support from your higher self. It grants you the ability to perceive beyond misconceptions to retrieve greater truths. The third eye considers everything that transpires from the perspective of witness consciousness or from being present. It allows you to view self-limiting concepts and cultivate wisdom that originates from a non-dualistic perception, transcending polarities such as good/bad or positive/negative. This helps you to recognize the profound implications of the circumstances of existence.

The right cerebral hemisphere's role is inventiveness and creativity. Wisdom and intelligence emerge from their combination with the left hemisphere's function with reason and analysis, mediated by the actuated third eye. As your center of integrity, this is where your principles and feelings of honesty begin. You see and grasp more profound concepts and messages when your third eye is fully open and balanced.

Your third eye chakra is connected with intensified psychic development since the brow region is associated with the eyes and visual sensory perception. It also is associated with the pineal gland, located posterior to your third eye chakra in the brain. As your powers flourish, you will feel a tingling sensation here. This chakra is responsible for increasing your intuition, bolstering your spiritual consciousness, and augmenting your clairvoyance ('second sight'). The third eye chakra's function is to help create your internal understanding, motivation, and genuine purposefulness.

Traditional tantric practices highlight the necessity to balance all other chakras before beginning the process of clearing and opening the third eye chakra. This creates the foundational capacity needed to manage visions and perceptions of your higher mindfulness. Opening the third eye chakra without proper preparation creates overwhelming sensory overload and causes otherwise avoidable difficulties.

Dolphins have telepathic powers that enable them to communicate through their third eye chakra with other cetaceans across the globe. Their sonar, clicking, and chatter open your third eye chakra. You do not have to be in the water with the dolphins to experience this — holding an image of a dolphin in your mind during meditation can begin opening your third eye chakra. Another method is to invite them to visit you in your dreams. Dolphins emanate divine love and wisdom. Frequently distinguished for their aspiration to communicate with humans, dolphins help you to connect to your higher self. Dolphins are spiritual influences that assist you in healing and encourage you to adopt an extra-loving vision of authenticity.

By balancing the chakras and allowing your third eye to govern and control them, you remain open to all the information they receive. Learning to balance the energies of the mind helps perceive, discriminate, and attain knowledge. These allow you to cultivate wisdom over time, which you can use to benefit the world around you.

29. Acknowledging the Divine

Appreciate your spirituality through introspection.

YOU ARE NATURALLY, exquisitely divine, whether you recognize this or not. This truth cannot be altered. Fear and separation have denied you the ability to appreciate your divinity. The message of this card is that the mystery of contentment is not to chase after what you lack. The secret is to gaze inward and accept your genuineness. This is your holiness. Anything else does not matter.

Located at the top of the head, the crown chakra is the final energy center found within your physical body. The Sanskrit name for the crown chakra, *sahasrara*, translates to 'one thousand petals' since it is thought to form a lotus flower with one thousand petals.

The vitality of the crown chakra is at the topmost section of your head, positioned like a crown, radiating upwards. It is said to be where your distinctive awareness encounters a higher state of universal consciousness, enabling you to experience spiritual growth and be connected to the broader Universe.

This chakra is accountable for the otherworldliness of your boundaries. When you are absorbed in the energy of your crown chakra, you feel a sense of idyllic harmony all around you. It allows you to move past worldly needs and to bond with your being as a whole. This chakra grants access to ultimate clearness and open-minded wisdom.

The crown is the connecting site between your physical body, your soul, and the rest of creation. This chakra is the heart of enlightenment and consciousness. When the crown chakra is harmonized, it brings outlooks of tranquility, joy, and deep peace.

Understanding your existence doesn't have to be impeccable to be distinct. The more time you spend aiming to create a reality that is unflawed, the fewer occasions you can devote to appreciating it. Human existence is perfectly flawed. Discover your divinity to appreciate imperfections as well as treasures. Pardon yourself for your shortcomings. Articulate your flaws and then enjoy those imperfections all the same. Doing this will make you feel more whole and content, lacking cravings and distracting desires.

Plant the seeds of encouraging thoughts. You can't switch off all your feelings — they show up independently. However, you can decide how you react to them. By tuning into the crown chakra, you are tuning into the heart of the Divine itself. When contemplating events or situations around you—or even your thoughts—the divine perspective is non-attached to these, seeing them all as part of the Universe.

Dolphins remind you to be no longer complacent with accepting the way things have happened or the life you have. They guide you to see the excellent prospect of consciously living your life. You have the power to do this now. The dolphins ascertain that you simply need to take your first step. This step will lead you to your higher self's path. Be willing to be the divine individual you are destined to be.

38. Access Your Enlightenment

When initiated, divine love, light, and peace are capable of pouring through this energetic center to enable your higher consciousness.

SOMETIMES IT MAY SEEM that our spiritual journey has no outcome, wandering blissfully and blindly through healings, awakenings, and openings without truly understanding what it is all for. Our higher consciousness connecting us to the Divine is a great plan that our soul understands. With each lifetime, our spirit gains new understandings. Your journey to enlightenment is the reason you are here. This card reminds you to connect to this purpose.

The soul star chakra is the eighth energy center and is situated above the crown chakra, extending anywhere from six inches to two feet above your head. It resides outside the physical body yet remains in the aura. Divine light flows upward through this chakra, uniting you to the unlimited influence of the divine love and light before flowing back down to replenish, enlighten, and empower your whole being. This is your soul — the point where transcendent energy passes into the physical body. When you connect your soul to your conscious mind, you can understand your soul's purpose and karma.

To attain this insight, there are some fundamental steps to take. Initially vigorous, each action taken will lead you closer to your goal. There will be setbacks, but these vary in intensity based on how committed you are to your progress.

Recognize the spiritual aspect of everyday life and choose to expand your awareness and develop your enlightenment. Once you make this determination, put in the time and effort to evolve your mind, body, and spirit until you understand the Universe is in a perpetual state of harmony. Be determined to achieve this harmony within yourself. Your soul becomes revitalized, and you begin to accept your spiritual wishes. Find the correct energy exercise—such as yoga, meditation, or qigong—and devote yourself to it conscientiously.

Live your life according to your values. Your practice will become more consistent as you attain better emotional, mental, and physical well-being. Over time, you generate new and more individualized methods of preparation.

The dolphins remind you that you are a spiritual being. Dolphins do not do anything for acknowledgment or to be the center of attention. The dolphin asks us to become mindful of helping others and be in service to others without seeking recognition. This is why the soul star chakra is called the seat of compassion. Assisting others is a way to hone your skills subtly and continually. Once you can complete actions from a place of love, you shift in your soul's growth. Attending to others is essential for moving through these steps. Assisting others is a sincere spiritual habit.

Make up your mind to accomplish enlightenment and persistently work toward developing your spiritual customs without simply appropriating the traditions of others. You can relate the practices of others to your existence but avoid following them slavishly. Take what works for you, and leave behind the dogmas and ideologies that make sense in their original cultural settings.

Enlightenment is something you practice continuously. It is imperative to care for your basic needs without relying on others. You clear away old energy by evolving through good intentions and efforts and following your integrity. However, you cannot wholly retain everything you obtain until you communicate it on your terms and redistribute your interpretation to those around you.

By tapping into the soul star chakra, you get closer and closer to attaining enlightenment and understanding the intention of living a human existence. Enlightenment has a greater purpose, and that is in bringing it into ordinary, everyday life. When you do this, you are coming closer to the Source, helping others find their connection to their highest selves, making their lives better, and creating harmony on the planet to heal all.

31. Surprise Encounter

Most of us experience day-to-day life as a relatively habitual, predictable series of circumstances. What this card suggests is something different altogether — those synchronistic, seemingly random events become bookmarks in the story of our lives. This happenstance could be an opportune meeting, something precious that is hidden, an instant attraction, a close call, coming across something exceptional, connecting with your angel or divine existences, or a surprise connection in a meeting with a dolphin.

  Surprise encounters can be unceremonious and unplanned interactions with people that sometimes happen by intention but often unexpectedly. Something about this meeting ignites a spark that leads to a surprising development. Informal meetings that generate a surprise encounter typically come from a

You will become familiarized with something or somebody in a synchronistic encounter.

weak connection, a connection with someone you wouldn't normally engage with creatively. In this encounter, you relax your guard and unexpectedly pursue their sentiments and participate with their perspective. In some way, the situation leads to an explorative engagement. When we are in a mindset of exploration and curiosity, we are more likely to conceptualize diverse chunks of information in a connecting way. The more we remain open to this, the grander the energy for visualizing something different to occur in our lives.

A hidden treasure can also be a blessing discovered at the close of every challenging situation. You essentially want to find the silver lining in these circumstances, as every hardship has a reward if you wait for it to show itself. A surprise encounter could be concealed at first but surfaces as a gift or some kind of indulgence or treat. It could also reveal itself as talents or parts of yourself that you have not yet discovered. It could be accessing your true self.

Surprises can show up in surreptitious ways. Be prepared—but not expectant—at any time for a surprise that may take your breath away, make you giggle, or enchant your inner child. A surprise is an awareness of a phenomenon you feel concerning the unforeseen. It is something that inspires attentiveness and stimulates your curiosity. The sentiment of wonder is commonly displayed by an open mouth and wide eyes, a physical reaction to amplified excitement and attention. Contrast this with our facial expressions when bored and disinterested — predictability results in condensed attentiveness and lessened excitement. The sense of surprise grabs our attention and piques our curiosity, so we are motivated to explore and discover something new.

    To many individuals, dolphins are just lighthearted mammals that enjoy swimming at the bow of a ship or in the wake of waves created by a traveling boat. The sensitivity, perception, love, and wisdom teachings they offer to humans stay concealed to those who have not yet exposed their hearts to the surprising gift beneath a dolphin's eyes. A dolphin might surprise you by appearing in your introspection or dreams.

32. Taking It All In

Accomplishment is contemplated in the eye of the observer; it is distinct for each individual.

AFTER A CHALLENGING period of struggle, you may have discovered that a prosperous life relies on how positive you are and includes your capabilities, the changes you've made, and how you've grown. Everyone has specific, individualized goals. Most people will choose to avoid the difficult route to success. This card tells you that you get to decide what you want to do and how to accomplish what you desire. Taking it all in allows you to fully assess where you are and where you would still like to go.

Learning is accentuated during novel involvements, and it is in these moments that growth is optimized. Instead of dreading the unfamiliar, affirm to yourself to participate in what lies before you and allow this opportunity to lead you along a new track. For example, don't only make choices based on money or financial aims as your objective — because there is so much more to life. It is not the only measure of success or accomplishment. When you take some time to reflect on what has been and may be approaching, trust and believe that money will flow into your life.

    We all tend to function at our best after moments of revitalization. This can be achieved in many ways: reading a book, taking a bath with mineral salts and essential oils, drinking a cup of warm tea, lighting a fragrant candle, volunteering at an animal shelter, sitting by an ocean or a lake, or going for a stroll in the park with a friend or close family member. Whatever it is that causes your heart to feel full, replenished, and loved, take some time for yourself. Even if what you choose appears small, create time for it. It is the little things we cherish that assist in preserving our sanity and happiness. When we make space in our lives to reflect on what is and isn't important, we prioritize the success of future accomplishments. Be willing to release anyone or anything currently in your life that does not make you feel supported, worthy, or loved. Allow yourself to try new adventures and enjoy the experience you gain.

    As you mature, you will reflect more on your life's choices — you get to choose what you will remember. As you develop and determine your life's goals, consider what moments you want to cherish. It is essential to recognize that you will receive tenfold the energy you place in the world. Giving positive energy and love to those around you will return positive energy and devotion. Always give your best to everyone and everything each day.

    To make a constructive impression on the earth and individuals close to you necessitates being accountable, dependable, and responsible for your deeds. Take a moment to evaluate and look at your situation from a bird's eye view. Consider what activities fill you with joy, and prioritize those. When you take on a task begrudgingly or from a sense of obligation, there is no benefit to anyone. When you commit to doing something, follow through on your word from a place of love and compassion. Take on projects you know you will achieve without creating stress or negativity on yourself or someone else.

Dolphins live very deliberately, even though it appears they are merely frolicking in a carefree manner. They give themselves space to make choices and are here to teach us that all good things take time.

Taking it all in is a deliberate act of creating space and ensuring your choices honor your integrity and truth and will lead to the success and achievement you desire.

33. Deep Plunge

A deep dive takes you into the very depths of your nature.

THE ENTIRE WORLD IS IN a unique period and beckons you to remember who you are and reflect or find solutions to your difficulties. You have visions for the pursuits and purposes in your life, and now is the perfect opportunity to contemplate your direction in life and how your plans are working out.

There are times when you feel the urge to dig deeper. Recognize that the world has changed, and you have transformed alongside it. Many have made drastic changes in their lives over recent years — in their jobs, homes, and even how they navigate the world around them. When you cannot go anywhere, obtain the reward by doing the deep inner work necessary to change and re-invent who you are. Consider your true nature, predispositions, and the ideas that inspire and stimulate your desires.

To begin your awareness and self-discovery journey, you'll

need to take a mindful approach to self-exploration. Minor changes to your contentment may not help to ease any sense of unproductivity or irritation you are experiencing. It's time to scrutinize your life and examine who you are more intensely to find the precise place to start or reset.

Negative situations impact your life and accumulate, creating a layer around your heart. Eventually, this accumulation builds up and renders it challenging to retrieve the genuineness that exists in you. To plunge to the depth you desire, you need to dive beneath these surface layers to the innermost aspects of yourself. All you need for fulfillment and happiness lies deep within you.

As you delve into the areas within you where previous pain, humiliations, upsets, and disenchantments dwell, you will find the truth of who and what genuinely stimulates the love inside you. You can decide to proceed deeper still. When you navigate beyond past experiences that stifled your emotional expression, you will rediscover your inner strength, power, sensitivity, and natural intuition. This is where your authenticity lives. Your heart is the superior guidance system that encourages you to construct your genuine life.

When you scrutinize yourself to these intensities, you can discover what you long to bring to the surface and what is necessary for you to release. When you know what resides underneath your amassed levels of junk, you can observe what was causing blockages and discomforts and understand the resolve they sustained. Frequently, the collected nonsense causes you to go further so that you can pursue your integrity.

Like a dolphin, dive into new ocean depths in search of food or to explore. It is vital to remember to resurface for air and that the purpose of a deep dive is to take you to your more extraordinary personality.

34. Bubbles of Protection

Bubbles represent techniques you have innately developed to shield yourself.

LOVE BUBBLES ARE created by your heart. What you do with your heart cannot be extinguished. The love you have generated in this life will always remain and form energetic bubbles. These bubbles are not only filled with your love, intentions, prayers, and good wishes, but they revolve in the vastness of space.

Dolphins travel in groups referred to as pods. While swimming closely together, they naturally form a bubble of protection that surrounds the entire group of dolphins. When you swim with dolphins, they lovingly surround you with bubbles filled with the energy of their light, joy, and love. Since the younger dolphins tend to mature slowly, pods offer them protection. The advantage of strength in numbers enables the dolphins to shelter the animals from sharks and other predators. Their message to you through this card is to guide you into creating protective spaces around yourself and your loved ones.

There are numerous methods to energize and shield yourself. These methods usually include constructing boundaries. For example, when you are in a challenging situation, you could physically take a step back. This action illuminates your respective space bubble and delineates your boundary. Another approach is pausing before speaking or acting to give yourself some breathing room, securing time to center yourself.

It can be challenging to create limits if you've not done so previously or if your boundaries have been disrupted in the past. Sometimes we justify this due to unhealthy lessons from early in childhood. Discovering how to love yourself may be the first action to recovering your boundaries. A powerfully unified awareness of identity is vital to your health, including physical, emotional, spiritual, and mental well-being.

One technique to feel resilient and safe consistently is to envision a protective bubble surrounding you. This is an effortless practice you can perform every day. Begin by sitting in a comfortable position. Place your hand on your lap, palms upward. Take a deep breath and imagine a bubble surrounding your body. Fill it with a color that will support you with whatever you desire at that time. For example, if you find blue calming, then use that for a bubble of peace. Your protective sphere may require a recharge throughout the day, such as entering or finding yourself in a particularly hard or perplexing situation. When that occurs, take a minute to bring mindfulness to your bubble and seal it with your appreciation of security, dominance, power, and peacefulness.

Like any new routine, learning to imagine and feel the existence of a protective bubble takes time and practice. After a few attempts, you will find it's not difficult and can be done in minutes. It's simply taking time to produce the image consistently every day. The more frequently you practice creating your protective bubble, the more naturally it will happen and the sturdier you will feel. If you have difficulty crafting this as a consistent routine, the exercise of loving compassion is an ideal approach to construct your self-worth so that you feel worthy of self-care and safety.

When this card appears in your reading, it is because your dolphin guides remind you to check on your boundaries and maintain them where necessary. And if you don't have any, look to them to discover how you can create your protective bubbles. Remember to always draw the energy for the bubble from your heart, your center. When you do this, you will only filter out what doesn't serve you, allowing a healthy two-way flow of loving energy to transfer between yourself and those around you.

35. Unforeseen Storms

35. Unforeseen Storms

COMPLICATIONS, problems, and discord may be clouding your happiness, like a storm over the ocean. No one likes the appearance of challenges, yet turmoil often presents a potent opportunity for personal growth and development. Things change continuously during a storm; just as it eventually passes, so will the difficulties in your life. Even in the darkest of times, the sun of clarification eternally shines above the concealed clouds. If you raise your realization high enough, you can learn to rise above what transpires. Being good to yourself by utilizing all your preferred energy-clearing methods, centering, and self-healing is how you weather the storm.

Unforeseen storms are a disturbance or innovative disruption that feels like the Universe kicking you out of relaxed complacency. The reorganization of your inner

Storms will always come and go to disrupt your life; learn to weather them by using tools that keep you centered, grounded, and loving.

mechanism usually brings a modification ultimately for good. It is a universal truth that things collapse when they become unsustainable, only to be renewed and restored. An individual's journey can include frequent difficulty as much as the experience of happiness.

In these situations, the stress can be so overwhelming that it wears down your positivity, and you're sure you cannot prevail over the problems in front of you. In reality, there is no condition so horrible, no trial so huge, and no option so incomprehensible that it cannot be conquered. Although you might think that all routes have been shut down to you or that your most diligent efforts will amount to nothing, you are never left without viable solutions and alternatives. The best course of action may be hidden within uncertainty, but the possibility exists. When you are honest with yourself concerning this simple fact, you can overcome anything because you will never stop looking for a solution to the challenges before you.

When you find yourself in the middle of the storm and feel you cannot even create a ray of happiness, take a moment to gather before trying to see the silver lining. Start merely with facing the problem head-on, knowing you've got to endure. Then decide to begin every day by conveying a positive tone. This is your power; you need the determination to encounter the transformations you want. Use whatever tools you have at your disposal — imagining what it will be like once you're past the challenges, encouraging yourself and others, journaling your experiences, or envisioning what you want. Simply set a positive attitude for your day. It all comes down to your mindset.

Everything in the Universe is aware, and your thoughts affect everything around you — including the storm itself.

When storms hit the seas, dolphins retreat to the shelter of nearby bays. They can dive deep into the water to withstand things but still need to come to the surface to breathe. They know they have to stick together and head for shelter — they don't have time to fret about the disruption to what they were previously doing.

Use all your skills to keep yourself together while you make your way out of the storm, and face the challenges as they present themselves. In this way, growth comes after the storm has passed, and you can reflect on what you experienced and learned and the improvement to whatever skills you employed.

36. Light Body

The light body is your means to progress from the human configuration to the form needed to return to the Source.

IF THE OBJECTIVE OF your being as an enlightened soul is to become one with the Universe, then the initiation of your light body is what advances you to expand toward this goal.

Your light body has several layers over the physical body. They are called energetic, astral, mental, and causal bodies. Talents and abilities beyond your five physical senses stem from your light body. Many spiritual traditions taught variations of this idea. Their sages understood that all things in existence are composed of energy. Solid matter is the condensing of energy-generating substances. Comprehending how to utilize form optimally was the work of sages and is now becoming the practice of the awakened collective.

When we feel confused, lost, depressed, and closed off from the world and ourselves, this indicates that the light body's various layers are disconnected and in disharmony. Eventually, we become so cut off that any prospect of evolution or returning to Source is denied. This card reminds you how to reverse this and to attain the light body. Unlock the body's subtle energy centers, by harmonizing and balancing the chakras and clearing the inner channels. This is like rewiring the body's electrical systems. There are several ways to do this.

Look after your physical body. This cannot be stressed enough — your physical body is the anchor of your light body to the human world. How this looks will be different for each individual. Essentially it means getting the appropriate amounts of quality rest. Eat according to your physiological needs, don't buy into fad diets or one-size-fits-all approaches, and eat reasonable amounts at proper times. This also includes minimizing toxic inputs but also mitigating their effects. Find a holistic doctor or health practitioner that understands your specific needs and follow their guidance.

Lighten your soul. Laugh more, listen to music you love, and surround yourself with what helps you feel most at ease. Surround yourself with people who feel 'light' and share in good times together. Whatever experience fills your heart with bliss helps expand your light. Spend time in nature, whether it's the forests, the beach, mountains, lakes, etc. Clean air and sunlight have been shown in studies to have tremendous benefits for physical and mental health. It also connects you spiritually to the Universe via other life forms experiencing a three-dimensional existence.

Live everyday life with truth and integrity. Be authentic. Be yourself. This might take time as you peel away layers of conditioned behaviors and beliefs, and the journey to uncover our true nature is the journey of becoming our divine, higher selves.

Chakra cleansing and clearing channels allow physical, three-dimensional energy to be integrated and interconnected through various light body levels. The main chakras are conduits to the layers of the light body. Nutrition, exercise, and human experience are transmuted and refined in the physical body into light energy channeled to the light body's layers.

When you do this, you will feel a sense of peace and well-being, increased awareness, increased intuition, heightened creative senses, and an increase in synchronicities.

A dolphin's energy is continuously light, brilliant, open, and sentient. Being in their presence either meditatively or physically supports you in opening to a superior vibrational frequency. Their light body is exceedingly advanced. The dolphins wish to assist in initiating and cultivating your light body to further you along the path toward ascension.

Attending to the needs of the light body not only helps you in this world but will lighten you in preparation for connecting to Source. The gifts that come with this are to benefit you and the world.

37. Auric Energy

Perceive auras and learn to manage your emotions.

THE AURA IS THE invisible otherworldly energy domain that encompasses all living phenomena. Everything thriving has auric energy. Dolphins have a beautiful teal-shaded aura. Similar to certain crystals and other pure forms of energy, dolphins' auras never change in color, nor do they need clearing. The distinctive colors of your aura are believed to convey the expression of your spiritual health.

When you long for vitality, lucidity, harmony, calmness, happiness, and health, consider learning about auras. As you discover the mechanisms of your aura, you will learn how to manage your emotions and energies.

The ability to discern how to fortify and purify your dynamic auric field is helpful for novices, expert psychics, and energy healers. When you train to visualize your aura, you inevitably engage your spiritual abilities and physical discernment to sense and perceive others' auras.

Everyone is born with the innate ability to perceive auras, but as they age and lose sight of their childlike imagination, they lose the capacity. Seeing auras is not deemed normal in Western cultures, so children mature, feeling their vision is impaired, stifling their gift. Learning to perceive auras is an act of unlearning or remembering what you once did.

Do you notice that you feel drained after interactions with someone? It could be that you are encountering a type of spiritual drain. Numerous psychics are hypersensitive and become sponge-like, hungering for external vitality sources. Learn how to replenish yourself, so you don't require energy from others. As you continue to work more frequently with your aura, you will acquire your psychic and spiritual boundaries, auric defense, and self-sufficiency.

Release any inflexible ideas that you have concerning what auras appear as. This may take some continual practice, and it is best if you approach seeing them from a relaxed and lucid place. Everyone has a unique experience when discerning them. Some individuals see gilded incandescence around beings and things, while others see hues or different echelons of colors and illumination. You may find you can see them better with your peripheral vision. However you learn to see it, an aura will be most observable at the center, located in the body's interior and radiating to an inch or two outside.

Not everyone can see aura colors with the unassisted eye. Some can feel them. Consider the different vibrations from positive and negative people — one warm and friendly, the other cold and unwelcoming. Before speaking a word, their energy can be felt. This vitality you sense in others is the presence of the aura.

Learning to perceive your aura is itself an act of developing self-awareness of your emotional state and how you project what you are feeling. When you are cognizant of how you feel, you can either change it or manage how you project it to others. Expressing your emotions is one thing — unconsciously sending them out to others through your aura is another.

This card is showing up to connect you with your own beautiful auric body of energy. Dolphins gently guide you to reflect on how you are feeling at this moment and recognize these emotions emanating from you.

38. Play

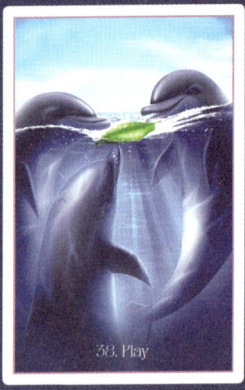

Sustaining awareness of imagination, originality, and enjoyment is associated with greater contentment throughout your life.

IT IS NATURAL TO encounter stress, but how you identify that pressure and whatever you do to handle it can leave a long-lasting impression on you. Play is believed to provide a robust and balanced spirit and benefits aging. One academic report established that individuals who regarded themselves as carefree and fun-loving found the difficulties of day-to-day existence more manageable.

There are numerous methods to be lighthearted, playful, and incorporate fun. Many individuals appreciate conversation and relaxing with family and friends. Others like substantial movement, exercise, and action. Your attitude is essentially more valuable than what you do.

Dolphins watch and repeatedly mimic each other, chase and frolic through the water, and create air bubble rings. Young dolphins learn how to play from their mothers. Although community learning among animals is not surprising, dolphins are exceptionally attentive mammals and appear to grasp actions quickly. This is more obvious if they are entertaining a group. Dolphins generate and control submerged bubble rings for play. They deliberately check the excellence of their circles and foresee their movements throughout playing. These delightful creatures are dedicated to their sport and can be seen playing with leaves they find drifting in the water. They will use their fins and noses to carry and pass a leaf to each other or play by themselves for extended periods.

Whether leaping out of the water, flipping into the air, slapping their tails, traveling throughout the water at high speed, or intermingling with other sea creatures, dolphins exhibit an element of playful comportment that signifies countless activities are purely for pleasure. They are considerably similar to humans, being exceedingly social and flourishing when with their community or family. Dolphins are talkative, compassionate, gifted marine mammals that perform unselfishly, assisting one another through their daily lives.

Bringing more play into your life is the lesson of this card. Activities such as being present, discovering pleasure in ordinary aspects, or noticing the enjoyment you feel when solving problems—such as brainteasers and games—are all types of play. Taking time to appreciate the world and its nuances is a characteristic attributed to playful people. When you are out in nature, allow yourself to experience what is being afforded to you. If it is raining, splash in a rain puddle. Build a sandcastle if you are on a beach. Lay in the grass, gaze up at the clouds and see what images you discover. Play is simply finding enjoyment, laughter, joyfulness, and recreation in your everyday living.

Follow the example of dolphins and use play to help you manage stress in your life. Spend more time laughing and being mirthful in your everyday life, and you will notice how much more energy you find. By being more playful with people around you—family, friends, work colleagues—you will bring about a greater sense of community that inevitably brings everyone closer together and working together toward common goals. A lighthearted attitude to daily life prepares you to manage the unavoidable pressures of life better.

39. Dream Time Visitor

39. Dream Time Visitor

Connect with dolphins in your dream time and retrieve messages and guidance.

DREAMS AND INTUITION reflect your receptiveness to extrasensory information. You can use this activity to understand a situation, including your finances, well-being, relationships, and life. With this card showing up, dolphins are swimming into your dream time to help awaken these senses, so you can receive the guidance you need at this time.

Working with sentient beings during your dream time is outside the tangible realm of facts and reality. Dream work is not a complete process — it is all-inclusive, symbolic, representational, and multi-faceted. To open this method of collecting knowledge, you want to be cognizant beyond your somatic intelligence, i.e., your ability to see, hear, taste, feel, and smell. You must be able to connect to your internal intelligence, which comes from information gleaned from your extrasensory faculties, which include clairvoyance (pure, inner sight), and claircognizance (inner knowing), clairaudience (pure hearing), and clairsentience (inner sensitivity leading to understanding). These are attached to the dream state in a complex manner involving the capacity to acknowledge and interpret symbolic metaphors.

    For many individuals, accessing your inner awareness is wholly unfamiliar and awkward. Much of what you encounter with dolphins in dreams is suggestive evidence, whereas most of us prefer to work with literal information and facts. Consequently, it is easy to ignore the precious communication you are obtaining consistently. But, this type of communication is straightforward, divine assistance originating from the center of your being.

    Developing these extrasensory skills can help you circumnavigate your life. You may have access to one of these modes of connecting, or you may have all of the various modes — it honestly doesn't matter. Believe you have whatever you need to go forward with self-assurance. Look all around you but use your innermost senses to complement what you perceive, similar to envisioning with your eyes wide open. Soften your gaze, see beyond the obvious and observe everything possible in your surrounding area. Be aware of any vibrant colors or sounds. Don't focus on one thing; let your mind drift and use your imagination. Pay attention to symbolism and keep a journal of your observations. Note what you find fascinating, and describe what you perceive, no matter how fantastical and absurd. You will begin to notice patterns emerge, and your message will become apparent to you in no time.

Dolphins are said to visit our dream time. Dolphins reside in a continuum that exists outside of human-perceived time and space. They do not rely on clocks or time zones. There are no border crossings in their experience. Time is continuity, and space is endless. The waterways on Earth are circular without a clear beginning or end site. Comparable to the water on Earth, your mind reveals unique and colorful images.

Some say that when you have a dolphin dream, you will encounter group gatherings and a fortunate period ahead. Others suggest that dreaming of dolphins relates to a forthcoming rough time and awareness of the vulnerabilities ahead. Generally speaking, dolphins exemplify the joy you discover in life. They represent energy, openness, grace, and sophistication — qualities that you may or may not be aware of.

In any case, dolphins visit you during your dream to bring you vital information and help you develop your inner intelligence. Learning to be more conscious of your dreaming teaches you skills that enable you to be more present and aware in everyday life. With this, you can confront any challenge that you are facing.

48. Sacred Water

Visiting a sacred site can be a valuable means of unlocking an aspect inside you that has persisted in being shrouded.

SINCE ANCIENT TIMES, humans have constructed sacred sites in locations guided by the earth's life force (such as on ley lines and energy vortexes) and directed by benevolent beings of light. It is because of this guidance that the sites considered sacred have extensively served as storehouses of wisdom, energy, and illumination that can be retrieved by anyone who ventures to them.

The desires that motivate seekers to congregate upon such sites differ from one individual to the next. Some desire spiritual self-actualization above all else. Others yearn for nourishment from the sacred site's vitality for illumination, healing, deep introspection, mindfulness, or comprehension of intelligence long forgotten.

Many cultures have recognized the sacred nature of water, be it a river, lake, spring, or sea. Wells, springs, and water from the ground or caves were portals to another realm. In ancient Greece, for example, a mortal could travel to Hades' underworlds via one of five rivers. In Celtic cultures, wells were the doorways. For many Indigenous Australian nations, the rivers and creeks are associated with the rainbow serpent that created the land and the people.

Because of water's associations with purification and healing, sacred sites were established around water sources. In the Judaeo-Christian tradition, water was used to baptize people — a ritual of spiritual rebirth. In India, the Ganges is the manifestation of the goddess who offers purification and healing to all who touch her waters. Even today, many people flock to hot springs for the revitalizing power of mineral salts they contain and depend on the water from underground aquifers to grow their crops, which provide them with life.

For cultures that dwelled alongside the sea and depended on it for food and other resources, dolphins were recognized as guardians and protectors of the waters. Many saw them as 'ocean people' and reincarnations of deceased ancestors. Stories abound of dolphins rescuing drowning sailors and pods shepherding whales back into the ocean after beaching.

When this card appears, dolphins are calling you to visit the nearby waters that are sacred to you. Perhaps you need to bathe and calm your nervous system or use water to purify and heal your spirit and body. Given the importance of water for all life on this planet, perhaps you are being called to protect the seas from pollution and mismanagement. It is time to be guided to a sacred site and do what you feel called to do. Allow the natural magic of this place to encompass you and draw out your natural magic, which has been forgotten or covered by layers of conditioning.

The sacred water sites are beckoning you from a distance, inspiring your creativity, and reverberating profoundly inside your soul. These sites have established an innate relationship with divine energies that support all existence. Throughout your journey, reiterate your purpose to receive whatever blessings are expressed to you throughout the sacred water sites you call on. Your sensitivity will support you in generating enduring connections with these waters so you may obtain harmony and influence from anywhere.

41. Joyous Vortex

DOLPHINS PASS THROUGH the energy vortexes found in the ocean, filling them with their innate joy. An energy vortex is a point on Earth—land or sea—a spinning epicenter of energy. They encompass more power than other ordinary locations. They occur at the junctures of different ley lines, the lines of physical energy that generate the Earth's electromagnetic field. They can be likened to chakras and are vital to the energetic health of the planet. The energy vortexes in the ocean require caretaking, balancing, and harmonizing, provided by dolphins, whales, and other forms of sea life. Just as you can heal yourself through balancing your chakras, you can assist the ocean and support her healing by bringing joyousness to such places.

Energy vortexes have potent spiritual advantages or are highly beneficial for various spiritual activities. Some vortexes convey a

Connect with energy vortexes with joy to maintain yourself and the planet.

sense of peacefulness, harmony, stability, and quietude. Others are thought to encourage individual contemplation, deep understanding, and a clear heart and awareness. Others still act as influential centers of objective or emotional renewal. Ley lines are also understood to have spiritual importance. While there is no definitive map of the earth's ley lines, they are distinguishable by linking sacred places. Regardless of their characteristics, all these sites enable visitors to experience a sense of connection with themselves and the Universe.

Dolphins are naturally joyous beings. They swim in and out of the numerous joy-filled vortexes found within the ocean. The water quality at these places is better, and there is a translucent shimmer to the vortex's opening. Dolphins frequent these areas to maintain the balance of the vortex and amplify and elevate its energy. The vibration of joy will remain in the vortexes indefinitely unless it is otherwise destroyed through some major happenstance of destruction, such as an explosion or becoming clogged with pollution.

This card tells you to find your inner joy and bring that delightful energy to an energy vortex somewhere on the planet. Ideally, it would be one close to you, as you are attuned to the natural power of the place you live. Firstly, find an energy vortex. Perhaps there is an ancient or sacred site you know of. These can be sites that people have been visiting for millennia and don't need to have any human constructions on or around them. Stunning natural landmarks such as buttes, hilltops, unique rock formations, or water sources are usually vortexes. Trust your intuition.

When you visit an energy vortex, the effect on your body is profound. You may experience a lightheaded or disoriented feeling or feel ungrounded. Another common experience is the desire for rest or sleep to allow the encounter with the vortex to integrate into your being. Energy vortexes may be an endowment from a superior power to bestow healing, transparency, reconciliation, and additional wonderful attributes that would be harder to achieve outside these potent locations. More importantly, bring your joy. The purpose is as much for the benefit of the planet as it is for what you need. Attending these sites is vital for maintaining harmony with the earth's energy grid.

You can also energetically call on dolphins and ask to be taken to their joyous vortex. This can be achieved in your dream time, meditations, or while swimming in the ocean. Dolphins do not need to be physically present with you as the energy of their light body can assist you in achieving this desire. Using their unique powers, you can join your energy to theirs and help maintain the ocean vortexes. You maintain your energy body and the planet by activating your joyousness.

42. Ride the Wave

Learn to be focused, relaxed, and present, no matter how the energy is flowing in your life.

DOLPHINS LOVE THE opportunity to ride in the wake of waves created by boats and can be seen jumping and leaping through the surf, skimming next to surfers. They share the feeling of exuberance when it comes to confronting gigantic waves. Like them, you can master riding the waves in your life, which is the lesson of this card.

So many changes are happening worldwide, and it feels overwhelming — like being tossed around by crashing waves. There is no point in resisting the way the energy is moving. You can't ride waves when you are trying to control their direction. Your attitude needs to be flexible, hardy, trusting, and cooperative.

Just as the waves in an ocean shift, so do your feelings. Similar to waves, your responses may be calm one instant and forceful and erratic in the next. Our emotions shift like tides. They express how our inner energies move in response to external stimuli. Powerful moods and impulses seem like they will never finish. Your mood intensifies, and you operate on compulsion. Expressing strong emotions in an unproductive or inappropriate way can cause the situation to be unhealthy for ourselves and possibly trigger responses in others that are not conducive to harmonious relationships. How you respond determines your experience, not the feelings themselves.

Consider how the dolphins swim in the ocean. They don't compete with the commanding ocean waves that come their way — they move with the tide, riding the physical rise of the water. Recognize that your sentiments will persist only fleetingly and then recede, like traversing on the surf like a dolphin. Learn to ride the waves, not fight them. This means acknowledging your feelings while you experience them.

While experiencing your emotions, refrain from judging them. They are an aspect of you and are only fleeting. Consider every time you have made it through a challenging reaction. It resolved itself. Recognizing uncomfortable feelings permits liberty from misery. Learn to ponder your sentiments like the deep sea. Moods arise in waves — some whitecaps are stronger than others but will cease.

If emotions express how the energy inside you is moving (or not), then experiencing your sentiments allows your body to respond accordingly. You may feel like jumping up and down or shaking your body. You may feel like screaming — in which case, do so into a pillow so as not to distress others in your vicinity. You may feel like dancing or even punching a pillow. These actions don't get rid of the emotions. Instead, they allow you to experience the energy, to go along with its movement until it naturally peters out, much like catching a wave and riding it in to the shore.

Once the wave has receded, you will experience a moment of presence and calm. This is when you can reflect, allow your inner intelligence to understand what happened and why, and learn from the experience. Perhaps you'll recognize triggers or develop strategies for dealing with challenges moving forward. You'll also feel more focused and confident to face the next set of incoming waves.

Remember, emotions—like waves—are a temporary condition. Whatever is occurring in your life now, you can face it and overcome it, becoming wiser and stronger from the experience.

43. Timing

There is a discipline to timing and how to get the utmost out of your life.

TIMING PLAYS A CRUCIAL role in achieving goals. You may credit success to providence (fate, the Universe, karma, etc.) and suppose it is something you have no power over, but it turns out you can control your timing — at any point in your life. The better you comprehend timing configurations and the science connected to them, the greater you can increase the chances of accomplishing your desired outcomes. When this card shows up in your reading, it is a call to become aware of how you pace yourself throughout the day and within tasks and to learn to regulate timing.

Timing has three phases — beginning, mid-point, and completion. The beginning is the moment of initiating the action. It is inherently inspiring as we start a new venture and have enthusiasm. Generally, individuals have more drive at the start of a day, week, or year. If you find that you have a tumultuous beginning, simply start over.

The halfway point can be challenging. It is the time when you may be inclined to encounter your respites. You often don't exert your best at the midpoint of a day. Yet, the halfway point can also be encouraging. The key is consciously choosing to generate determination, whether in a day, in a venture, or even in a generation. Remember what your objective is and commit to seeing it through to completion.

How you finish something has a long-lasting mark on your awareness and how the project is understood and remembered. Keeping up the energy to finish is important so you can be proud of the result once completed. It can be somewhat easier to get through this phase, as the goal is within view, which motivates us.

There is a rhythm to timing to get the utmost out of your life. Notice your energy in each of the three phases mentioned above — what is it like at the start of your day or a project, how does it change midway through, and do you have the energy to complete it? Be aware of your inner regulator and take the time to select pauses and rests appropriately — is there a better time when a break invigorates you into the next phase?

Taking the time to become aware of your timing will indicate why you behave as you do and how they link to the ebb and flow of your energy. Even if you are the type of person who feels they don't need routines in their day, you will still discover an understanding of your natural rhythms. In Traditional Chinese Medicine, for example, there is a system of understanding the flow of *Qi* (energy) as it cycles through the different organ systems over 24 hours, making some times of the day more conducive to specific activities such as meals, rest, and physical exertion.

Dolphins exist utilizing divine timing. They follow a schedule concerning where and when they will hunt. They also follow a consistent pattern of when they will rest. Generally, dolphins can be found swimming in a specific bay at the same time regularly. They go with the energetic ebb and flow of the ocean, slowing them to fluctuate as needed without concern or stress to the types of constraints humans have constructed around time.

While we still need to honor the timelines of others we interact with, understanding our natural rhythms and timing helps us live and act with greater alignment with our authentic selves. You will find you will have more energy to begin and complete tasks and projects and sustain yourself with greater efficiency and vitality. Like dolphins, you will know when an activity is appropriate at any given time and be able to utilize the proper resources. You will also become more attuned to others' rhythms and learn to synchronize with them, making relating and working with others more harmonious and fruitful, which helps form communities that thrive. Timing is thus an integral piece of the inter-relatedness of all living things and the planet.

44. Trust

Trust presents a quiet hopefulness that miracles and boundless phenomena can happen at any moment.

TRUST IS WHAT YOU LEAN on to embrace repeatedly during a predicament, a severe illness, or difficulty. It sustains you when you are in dire conditions or any frightening circumstance. It helps reassure you that you are protected and safe no matter what happens. Trust is powerful and creates a positive vibration within, which benefits self-healing. This card reminds you to trust your intuition and your inner guidance to help you on your life path. It reminds you constantly to honor that deeper knowing from within, for to ignore it brings you out of balance and alignment with the authentic flow of your life.

Dolphins use echolocation to 'see' through water — a sonic frequency that bounces off objects and creates a type of 'picture' or vibrational sensation of physical objects in their field. This sixth sense is what helps them find food, alerts them to danger and helps them safely navigate their way. Dolphins know which things are sentient and which are inanimate. They know what to avoid and what to embrace. In essence, they trust their senses and the information gleaned from them.

Many sensitive people feel energetic vibrations, emotions, and feelings around them, picking them up using their inner antennae. This is the beautiful gift of being human, and the spirit of dolphins' trust can inspire you to fine-tune. They invite you to learn discernment between what you are meant to engage with, what you are told to ignore in life, and what is suitable for you and what is not.

Train your mind to trust what all your senses tell you — especially the non-physical senses. Just as love and fear cannot coexist, trust and fear do not reside with each other. Clear away your fear and remember to trust by taking a deep, abdominal breath to assist you with becoming calm and centered. When you do this, you shift from a negative mindset to a place of tranquil trust through prayer and meditation. You will also shift energetically by visualizing yourself as strong and surrounded by beings of love, such as angels and spirit guides. Envisioning this support can bring you blessings, renewed peace, and the gentle calmness associated with the feeling of trust.

When you walk through the world with trust, it acts as a force field that protects you from anything that brings harm. Of course, there will be moments when your guard is down, you get hurt, or a choice goes awry. When this happens, keep trusting. It isn't that your sense of trust was 'wrong' or that you can't hear that inner voice. Look for what you can get out of these situations and the lessons that can be learned. Your inner senses didn't lead you to this situation to fail — there was something important you needed. Trust that there is something positive and creative you can take from this.

Ultimately trust is part of living a conscious life of joy. Like dolphins, we should live to trust ourselves, trusting the community we surround ourselves with and that our senses will never lead us astray.

Afterword
by Ally Thompson

Angela Hartfield was a truly magnificent woman. She was full of laughter, joy, and love. She was the pillar of strength and wisdom for our family. After a 12-year battle with cancer, she unfortunately finally succumbed to her illness. We lost a treasure on October 5, 2021. Her spark for life was undeniable as she lived as if nothing was ever guaranteed. When I think of my mom, I can't help but think of all the laughter. She understood something more than the rest of us: that life is beautiful and meant to be enjoyed. Even when there was hardship, Mom found a way to carry on. She was a beacon of grace, wisdom, truth, and strength. In the last moments of her life, she still exuded all of this. Which is why it seems there is such a massive void without her. She was truly everything to us.

All of Mom's decks are special and I find comfort in being able to hear her voice in each message. This deck, however, will hold a special place in my heart, as I feel she continues to live through these cards and her words. Not a day will go by when she is not remembered for her playfulness, for her advice, for her love, and for all that she brought into our lives. We are blessed beyond measure to have been a part of her journey. Mom's deepest desire was to be in service and help others. She wanted to aid others in connecting to the Divine. I find happiness in knowing that she is now able to help so many more people all at once.

There is something magical about the fact that this is the last deck she wrote. She managed to write this while none of us had the real understanding that she was actually living her final days. I find it so appropriate that her final deck celebrates the playful, yet sage, dolphin. She was a lot like a dolphin. She wasn't of this world, really. She lived through joy and amusement. She was always unafraid to be true to her heart. I hope we can all continue her legacy by living life as she did — like it is truly a gift to be here.

About the Author

ANGELA HARTFIELD embodied the essence of a psychic medium, an internationally renowned spiritual intuitive reader and healer, as well as an esteemed teacher. Her profound connection with the angelic realm radiated through her empowerment-focused techniques, guiding individuals in harnessing assistance and guidance from both angels and the Universe itself.

Angela's spiritual journey commenced with an angelic encounter at the tender age of four, igniting her lifelong communion with the spiritual realm. This innate connection fueled her mission, leading her to establish the Angelic Channeler Course (ACC), a prestigious certification program based in Tokyo, alongside numerous workshops that unfolded in her beloved home state of Hawai'i. Among her notable offerings was a class dedicated to Hawai'ian Healing Journeys, showcasing her holistic approach to healing.

Her creative brilliance shone through the decks of oracle cards she meticulously crafted. *The Angelic Whisper Oracle Cards*, *Whispers of Love Oracle Cards* (centered on love relationships), *Nature's Whispers Oracle Cards* (focusing on nature's embrace), *Whispers of Lord Ganesha Oracle Cards*, *Whispers of Healing Oracle Cards*, *Whispers of the Ocean*, and *Whispers of Aloha* were testaments to her insight and spiritual wisdom, all available through Blue Angel Publishing.

Angela's legacy extended beyond her teachings. Her meditation CDs, including *Finding Your Life Purpose — A*

Meditation with Archangel Raziel and the Humpback Whales and *The Magical World of Fairies*, resonated with clients across the globe, aiding them on their journeys of self-discovery.

While she graced far-flung corners of the world with her teachings, Angela found her heart's center in Kailua Kona, Hawai'i, where she crafted her inspirations. As a devoted mother of four remarkable daughters and a stepson, Angela's nurturing spirit extended beyond her professional endeavors. She and her husband, Duke, shared a profound passion for the ocean and diving, cementing their bond as PADI Certified Dive Masters.

For a deeper exploration of Angela's profound contributions and her rich tapestry of experiences, visit her website: **www.angelahartfield.com**

About the Artist

EKATERINA GOLOVANOVA emerges as an exceptional and multi-talented graphic artist, illustrator, and designer hailing from the vibrant city of Moscow, Russia. Her artistic journey began at a young age, kindling a passion that led her to a children's drawing studio, where her creative spark first ignited. Graduating from art school served as a foundation for her subsequent pursuit of higher education at the prestigious Moscow State University of Printing Arts, Faculty of Graphical Arts.

Within her dynamic career, Ekaterina not only thrives as a distinguished designer but also flourishes as a sought-after freelance illustrator. Her insatiable curiosity has driven her to explore diverse fields of knowledge. Delving into studies at the International School of Vedic Astrology Rami, she embraced the depths of various subjects. Notably, her recent accomplishment in Counseling with Metaphorical Associative Maps not only attests to her dedication but also unveils her boundless creativity. This achievement has inspired her to craft her own captivating decks of cards, a testament to her imaginative spirit.

For a glimpse into Ekaterina's awe-inspiring artwork and creative universe, you can find her at: **www.GALEKA.ru** or on Instagram: **@galekaek**

Also available from Blue Angel Publishing®

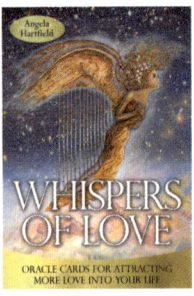

WHISPERS OF LOVE
Oracle Cards for Attracting More Love into Your Life

Angela Hartfield
Illustrated by Josephine Wall

Whispers of Love was created to help you find methods and messages for building stronger, more loving relationships whilst also to remind you of the interconnectedness of everything in your life. Whether it be a romantic connection or your connection to others around you, these beautifully illustrated cards will help you find answers and solutions. You can choose cards for everyday guidance or you can do readings focusing on a specific question or relationship. However you use these cards, they will be an invaluable tool to add clarity to your situation by connecting you with your inner guidance and intuition.

50 cards and 76-page guidebook set • ISBN: 978-1-922161-10-9

Also available from Blue Angel Publishing®

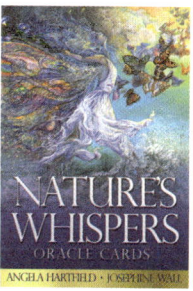

NATURE'S WHISPERS ORACLE CARDS

Angela Hartfield
Illustrated by Josephine Wall

Nature is continually enticing us to spend time in her embrace, through the calling of birds, the babbling of brooks and streams, the fragrant smell of the flowers and the whispers of the trees as the wind blows through their branches.

Through this vibrant deck, featuring the exquisite artwork of Josephine Wall, nature beckons you to experience a world of profound beauty and timeless wisdom.

Re-ignite your connection to the great spirit of Mother Earth and tap into the profound peace, healing and guidance she offers us – if we only take a moment to listen.

50 cards and 72-page guidebook set • ISBN: 978-1-922161-39-0

Also available from Blue Angel Publishing®

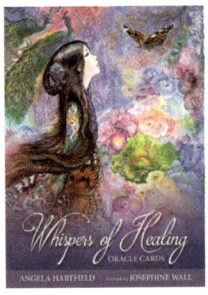

WHISPERS OF HEALING ORACLE CARDS

Angela Hartfield
Illustrated by Josephine Wall

Whispers of Healing is here to help you nourish, strengthen and restore yourself to emotional, physical, and spiritual wellness. Whether you wish to heal a broken heart, resolve a work challenge or discover ways to fine-tune your beliefs and attitudes, this deck is ready to journey by your side as a source of support, guidance and insight.

Turn to this oracle whenever your health seems compromised, and the soothing energy and wisdom will help you navigate your way to balance, wholeness and wellness. It is time to unlock true, deep and complete personal healing.

50 cards and 88-page guidebook set • ISBN: 978-1-925538-26-7

Also available from Blue Angel Publishing®

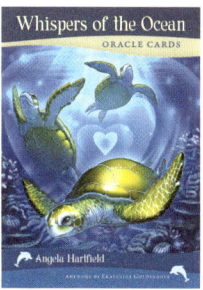

WHISPERS OF THE OCEAN ORACLE CARDS

Angela Hartfield
Artwork by Ekaterina Golovanova

Enjoy the flow and master the currents of your life with playful dolphins, patient seahorses, regenerative starfish and other fascinating marine beings. Ask a question and tap into the intelligence and grace of our planet's rich, healing and revitalising oceans for divination, direction, and decision-making.

This sumptuous new collaboration from Angela Hartfield and Ekaterina Golovanova delves beneath the surface and connects you with ancient, knowing, and wondrous companions so you can draw on greater strength, replenish your reserves, turn the tide on uncertainty, and emerge with clarity, purpose, and confidence. *Whispers of the Ocean* will help you ride the waves of life so you can come out on top.

50 cards and 124-page guidebook set • ISBN: 978-1-925538-73-1

Also available from Blue Angel Publishing®

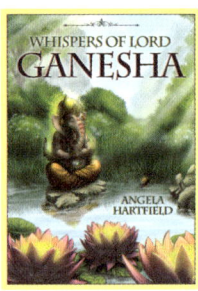

WHISPERS OF LORD GANESHA

Angela Hartfield
Artwork by Ekaterina Golovanova

Lord Ganesha, the renowned elephant-headed god, is one of the most revered and worshipped deities in the Hindu pantheon. Ganesha's energy has the power to clear obstacles, bestow wisdom, and promote prosperity and success in all ventures.

Work with this unique deck to invoke the blessings and protection of Lord Ganesha, patron of the arts and sciences and keeper of great knowledge. Call on him whenever you feel yourself in need of inspiration, guidance, and a clear path through the obstacles and challenges that lie ahead.

50 cards and 96-page guidebook set • ISBN: 978-1-922161-93-2

Also available from Blue Angel Publishing®

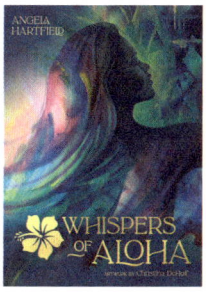

WHISPERS OF ALOHA

Angela Hartfield
Artwork by Christina DeHoff

Embrace the bliss, empowerment, and spirit of Aloha through Angela Hartfield's oracular ode to her island home. In her signature style, Angela illuminates the wisdom within the artworks, so they convey personal meaning for detailed and revelatory readings. The lush imagery by Maui-based Christina DeHoff provides a visual connection to the elements, deities, nature, and joys of Hawai'i. Revel in glorious inner and outer landscapes, dance where worlds meet, and immerse yourself in wonder as you discover direction, guidance, purpose, and harmony.

With a Foreword by Alana Fairchild.

44 cards and 160-page guidebook set • ISBN: 978-1-922573-46-9

For more information on this
or any Blue Angel Publishing® release,
please visit our website at:

www.blueangelonline.com